General Washington's Army (1)

1775–78

Marko Zlatich • Illustrated by Peter F Copeland

Series editor Martin Windrow

First published in Great Britain in 1994 by
Osprey Publishing, Elms Court, Chapel Way, Botley,
Oxford OX2 9LP, United Kingdom.
Email: info@ospreypublishing.com

ISBN 1 85532 384 2

Series Editor: MARTIN WINDROW
Filmset in Great Britain
Printed in China through World Print Ltd.

FOR A CATALOGUE OF ALL BOOKS PUBLISHED BY
OSPREY MILITARY AND AVIATION PLEASE CONTACT:

The Marketing Manager, Osprey Direct UK,
PO Box 140, Wellingborough, Northants,
NN8 4ZA, United Kingdom.
Email: info@ospreydirect.co.uk

The Marketing Manager, Osprey Direct USA,
c/o Motorbooks International, PO Box 1, Osceola,
WI 540120-0001, USA.
Email: info@ospreydirectusa.com

www.ospreypublishing.com

Dedication

The author and the artist wish to dedicate this book to
our loving and supportive wives, Nancy and Moira.

Acknowledgements

We gratefully acknowledge the creative consultation
offered by Donald W. Holst, the contributions of
Captain Fitzhugh McMaster, Eric I. Manders, L. W.
Vosloh and James M. Kochan; the indispensable co-
operation of the staff of the division of Armed Forces
History, National Museum of American History,
Smithsonian Institution, particularly of Harry Hunter
and especially of Donald E. Kloster, and the help of
Kathleen Betts of the Society of the Cincinnati
Museum.

INTRODUCTION

During the period 1775–78, General Washington commanded three separate armies: the New England Army of 1775; the one-year Army of the United Colonies, renamed Army of the United States in July 1776; and the forces established by the Continental Congress to serve for three years from January 1777, or for the duration. Throughout the American Revolution, the rebel armies consisted of regular troops paid for by the Congress and of militia, volunteers and regulars raised by the states. This study focuses on the systems used by state and Continental authorities to procure clothing materials, the quantities they obtained and the specifications of the uniforms themselves.

The text illustrations include examples of typical arms and accoutrements used by the regular and state forces. A unique feature of this volume is the publication of monochromes of the Smithsonian Institution's collection of military clothing from the period 1775–78. Selected portraits and graphics rendered between 1775 and 1778 illustrate some of the adopted designs. The Plates show many of the distinct uniforms of volunteer companies, Continental regiments of 1776, provincial regulars, light horse, artillery, additional Continental foot regiments, Continental Line at Valley Forge, and independent Continental corps.

The subsequent volume in this series, *General Washington's Army 2: 1779–1783*, will complete this overview of the history of American military uniforms of the Revolutionary War.

George Washington 1776, by Charles Willson Peale (1741–1827). The uniform – blue with buff cape, lapels, cuffs, waistcoat and breeches – was made for him in 1775, probably modelled on the Fairfax (Virginia) Independent Company, which Washington commanded when he was named Commander-in-Chief in July 1775. Buttons and epaulettes are gold. The ribbon is light blue. (Dick S. Ramsay Fund, Brooklyn Museum)

COLONIAL UNIFORMS

Lacking the authority needed to raise regular forces, each of the 13 original colonies of North America, except Quaker Pennsylvania, enacted laws to establish a militia. With the exceptions of New York and South Carolina, no colonial militia law specified uniform clothing; however, each militiaman was supposed to maintain a usable fire-lock, ammunition and a bayonet. Officers were required to maintain a sword.

Owing to limitations in the militia laws, the colonists could only improve their proficiency in the military arts by forming volunteer companies. From 1774, they designated certain militia companies as minutemen – these companies were to be available for service at a minute's notice. Nominally part of the militia, minutemen were equipped and financed by direct local subscription. Independent companies found their own arms and equipment, and each adopted a uniform and established their own training programme.

Although the militia-based organisations enjoyed initial military successes, the committees of safety could not field viable forces without creating new formations that were enlisted for longer terms. In order to achieve this during 1775 and 1776, the provinces enacted legislation to raise provincial regulars, and appropriated funds to buy material for their clothing. On entering the service of the Continental Congress, many provincials were already in uniform.

Massachusetts

In planning a permanent New England Army, on 23 April 1775, the Massachusetts Provincial Congress resolved that a coat should be given to each soldier as a uniform. A Committee of Supplies was charged with responsibility for collecting and distributing shirts, breeches, stockings and shoes, and following inquiries from General Washington on 16 August, the council ordered the coats to be shortened so that they could be worn under hunting shirts as waistcoat without lapels. The number of the regiment was to be displayed on the pewter buttons. By 28 December 1775, around 13,000 uniforms had been made by the people of Massachusetts. At this time Massachusetts had raised 27 regiments.

As a major American port of entry for imported cloth whose inhabitants were skilled at making clothes, Boston began to receive imported and captured cloth and clothing. Boston also became a centre for the making of clothing for the Continental Army. A Continental Clothing Store was

Grenadier of the Grenadier Company, New York Independent Forces This unique portrait of an enlisted man in a colonial uniform is thought to depict General McKinney.

(Smithsonian photograph, printed by permission of the owners, Mr. and Mrs. Robert C. Pangborn of Bloomfield Hills, Michigan)

opened in Boston in 1777 and then transferred to Springfield in 1778. Massachusetts also boasted a well-established minuteman service and a considerable force of uniformed militia.

Known uniforms were as follows: Salem Rangers – short green coat, gold trim, cap of black beaver with four ostrich feathers, white under dress, black gaiters, ruffles at the wrist; Haverhill Artillery – blue faced buff, buff waistcoats and breeches, yellow buttons, white stockings; Boston Independent Company – black faced red; buttons with the motto '*Inimica Tyrannis*' and the device of a hand holding a drawn sword with the scabbard thrown aside and broken; white waistcoat, breeches and stockings, black half gaiters and feathers, black hats and black cockades; Pittsfield Minute Company – blue coats turned with white; Reading Minute Company – paper caps resembling those worn by British grenadiers; 3rd Bristol County Militia Regiment – officers in blue coats faced red, blue breeches, white stockings, yellow buttons and gold laced hats; Volunteer Company of Matrosses, 1st Hampshire County Militia Regiment – blue faced red, white small clothes, short black gaiters, black fur caps with red cockades; officers had red plumes.

Connecticut

During 1775, the Connecticut General Assembly raised eight provincial regiments. While clothing was not considered a necessity each regiment was allowed a coloured standard: 1st yellow; 2nd green; 3rd scarlet; 4th crimson; 5th white; 6th azure; 7th blue; and 8th orange.

For the campaign of 1776, Connecticut raised eight unnumbered regiments. Each regiment was responsible for obtaining its own uniforms. On 17 July, the Governor and Council of Safety resolved to supply enough home-made cloth of brown or cloth colour for 3,000 coats and waistcoats, 3,000 felt hats, checked flannel or linen for 6,000 shirts, and 6,000 pairs of shoes. On 2 October 1776, the General Assembly agreed to provide clothing for the eight regiments for the next three years. In a letter of 16 December 1776, Daniel Tillinghast, the agent at Providence, instructed Samuel Gray of Windham to make uniforms from cloth that had been bought in Providence from the prize ship *Thomas*. Uniforms were to consist of double breasted 'waistcoats' with lapels of the same cloth stitched down to the body, buttons set without button holes, a small matching cape, short plaited skirts, and sleeves with a small cuff. A jacket was to be worn under this waistcoat. The colours of these garments are described in the section dealing with Connecticut Uniforms on page 34.

Known uniforms were as follows: 1st Company, Governor's Foot Guards of Hartford – scarlet faced black, buff waistcoats and breeches, black fur grenadier caps; 2nd Company of New Haven – for detail see Figure 3 Plate A; Mansfield Militia – grenadiers in blue coats, scarlet waistcoats, white breeches and stockings, scarlet caps striped and tasselled with white, rank and file in white stockings and light blue cockades; Wethersfield Company – uniforms of blue turned-up red.

Rhode Island

On 6 May 1775, three regiments were authorised from among the various county militia companies. These troops marched to Boston carrying provincial blankets and knapsacks, but were otherwise self-clothed and equipped.

The cocked hat worn by Colonel Jonathan Pettibone of the 18th Regiment, Connecticut Militia, c.1775/6. Made of black wool felt with a small admixture of rabbit fur. It is 20 $\frac{3}{4}$ inches in diameter, with a 5 inch high crown, and edges bound with $\frac{3}{4}$ inch wide black silk. (Collections of the Division of Armed Forces History, National Museum of American History, Smithsonian Institution)

During 1776, the 1st and 2nd Regiments became the 9th and 11th Continental Regiments, and two state regiments were also raised for one year. On 23 July 1776, the General Assembly appointed a committee to procure clothing for its Continental troops, but its efforts did not bear fruit until 1777. Independent company distinctions were as follows: Cadet Company of Providence – scarlet coats faced yellow; Independent Troop of Horse, Captain-General's Cavaliers – blue coats faced white, yellow buttons, white jackets and buff breeches; Providence Grenadiers – black leather mitre caps with red backs and a flap on which was painted a gold lion, a gold anchor and edges, and silver scrolls with the words 'God and our rights' and 'Hope'; Newport Light Infantry – distinctive cap with a conical crown made from black leather, the rear turn-up was painted black with gold edging (see illustration below); United Train of Artillery – deserters in 1776 wore brown faced red. A black leather cap with an anchor on the front is associated with this unit.

New Hampshire

On 20 May 1775, the Provincial Congress resolved to raise, but not arm or equip, three regiments to join the New England army. On 21 January 1776, the Committee of Safety issued orders to raise and equip a regiment of rangers under Colonel Timothy Bedel for Continental service in Canada. Among the materials to be bought for this regiment were moose skins for moccasins, 500 pairs of shoes, 720 pairs of snowshoes, 688 blankets, and coarse cloth for Indian leggings, shirting and coats. The three regular Continental regiments raised as New Hampshire's quota were drawn from the militia and from New Hampshire men already serving in the Continental Army in November 1776. Their Continental uniforms are described below.

New York

At the request of the Continental Congress, on 27 June 1775, the New York Provincial Congress authorised four infantry battalions and one artillery company for Canadian service. The following day, Peter T. Curtenius, the state commissary, was ordered to purchase material to make up coats for these troops, and the day after that, the Provincial Congress instructed him that each regiment was to have different cuffs and facings. These four battalions were among the most elaborately uniformed provincial troops at this time, with tape to distinguish drummers' and fifers' coats, laced shoulder straps to distinguish sergeant majors and drum majors, pewter coat buttons with battalion numbers, waistcoat buttons displaying the NY cypher, russia drilling breeches and waistcoats, and narrow brimmed black hats. For the Canadian winter they also had

buckskin waistcoats and breeches, woollen leggings, mittens and caps. Regimental uniforms worn until November 1775 were as follows: 1st Regiment – blue faced scarlet; 2nd Regiment – blue faced crimson; 3rd Regiment – variety of colours faced green; 4th Regiment – variety faced blue; New York Artillery Company, commanded by Captain John Lamb – blue coats faced buff, 57 racoon caps were also received in Montreal; Green Mountain Boys – coats of green faced red.

The Provincial Congress decided to import cloth suitable for soldiers' shirts and coarse stockings by employing two or more ships to sail to Europe, obtain the cloth and sail it to St. Eustatius or St. Martin in the West Indies. There it would be off-loaded and picked up by other ships. By 30 April 1776, they had bought 4,393 yards of cloth, 12,869½ yards of linen, 2,861 hats, 473 shirts, 4,711 pairs of shoes and 966 gross of coat buttons.

During 1776 New York raised four additional battalions for its own defence. Having no suitable cloth, for hunting frocks, these battalions wore coats, leather waistcoats and breeches, hats, shirts, woollen hose and shoes. Uniforms worn by Colonel John Lasher's Battalion of Independent Companies of Foot were as follows (all wore white under clothes, half gaiters and black gaiters): Fuziliers – blue faced red, bearskin caps and pouches with a brass plate bearing the word 'Fuziliers' on the cap and

Side view of the cap worn by the Newport Light Infantry Company. The cone-shaped crown is made from a single piece of black dyed leather. The rear turn-up, like the front, is painted black with gold edging. (Smithsonian Institution)

'*Salus populi suprema Lex est*' on the pouch; German Fuziliers – blue faced red, silver lace, bearskin caps with white plates bearing the words 'German Fuziliers' and a tin star above; The Union – blue faced red; Sportsman – green faced crimson, small round hats; The Corsicans – short green coats, small round hats cocked on one side with a red tin heart bearing the words 'God and our Right', and around the crown 'Liberty or Death'; Bold Foresters – short green coats, small round hats turned-up on one side and with a brass plate on the front bearing the word 'Freedom'; Light Infantry – blue faced red; Oswego Rangers – blue coats, and small round hats with a brass plate against the crown bearing the words 'Oswego Rangers'; Rangers – green faced buff, buff waistcoat and breeches, white stockings, and black garters and half gaiters.

Other New York militia uniforms were as follows: Schenectady Minute Companies – one company of blues and one company of greens; Albany County Troop of Horse – blue coats, white buttons and silver laced hats; King's County Troop of Horse – blue coats, red jackets and silver laced hats.

New Jersey

On 3 June 1775, the New Jersey Provincial Congress recommended that each township form and arm a company of 80 men. The Committee of Safety recommended that minutemen companies wear hunting frocks. On 9 October 1775, the Continental Congress asked New Jersey to provide uniforms for two regular regiments for a year. Instead of a bounty, the privates were allowed a felt hat, a pair of yarn stockings and a pair of shoes. For its part, Congress agreed to furnish each man with a hunting shirt and a blanket; however, these were not to be considered as part of the terms of enlistment. Two more foot regiments were added to the state's line in 1776, and an ordinance for raising two companies of state artillery was passed by the Provincial Congress in March 1776. Known uniform details are as follows: Robert Erskine's Independent Company of Foot – green coats; 1st and 2nd New Jersey Regiments (1775–76) – hunting frocks.

Delaware

Delaware placed the militia on a rebel footing in May 1775 by appointing new officers and issuing detailed uniform regulations. A single Continental battalion was authorised by the Delaware Committee of Safety on 9 December. Uniform details were: Dover Light Infantry (1776–77) – green faced red; 2nd Kent County Militia Battalion (1775) – brown faced white; Light Infantry – blue faced white; New Castle County Militia (1775) – for details of this unit see Figure 1, Plate A; Haslett's Continental Battalion (1776) – according to Colonel Haslett's account book and deserter descriptions, blue coats faced red were worn.

Pennsylvania

Rather than accept militia, Quaker Pennsylvania's House of Assembly approved *Articles of Association of Pennsylvania* in August 1775; under these some 46 local battalions of Associators were formed. To ensure Pennsylvania's own defence, on 16 October 1775, the Council of Safety created a company of artillery under Thomas Proctor, and, on 5 March 1776, two state regiments: the Pennsylvania State Regiment of Riflemen and the Pennsylvania State Battalion of Musketry. On 5 October 1776, the two battalions were consolidated into the Pennsylvania State Regiment. Uniform details were as follows: Rifle Regiment – blue faced white, white waistcoats edged with red, buttons engraved with the letters

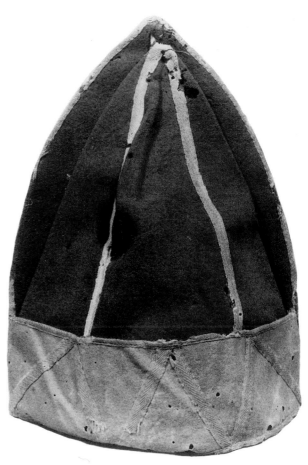

Grenadier mitre cap, 26th Continental Infantry Regiment, 1776. This view shows clearly the straw yellow $3\frac{1}{4}$ inch rear turn-up. The herringbone pattern $\frac{3}{4}$ inch white lace is sewn on in a zig-zag. The back of the front plate and the bag are made of wool in brown – probably the colour of the coat. (Smithsonian Institution)

PRB, black caps marked 'PR', lead coloured fringed hunting shirts; Musketry Battalion – blue faced red, white waistcoats, buckskin breeches, hats bound yellow; State Regiment – blue faced red, white small clothes, buttons with the inscription 'PSR'.

The *Associators'* uniforms were left to their localities, but the state regular forces came under the direct control of the Council of Safety, who appointed Francis Towers as the Commissary of Military Stores. Unless otherwise noted, all regiments wore white belted vests and breeches, white stockings, half boots, black garters and small round hats with fur cockaids. Regimental details were as follows: 1st Regiment – brown faced buff, red waistcoats and brown breeches; 2nd Regiment – brown coats faced red; drummers and fifers scarlet coatee with a brown collar, a blue hat ribbon and a buckstail; 3rd Regiment – drummers and fifers wore white faced brown; one buff taffeta and one Persian blue colour; Light Infantry Company – green with white lapels, jockey caps and feathers; 4th Regiment –

brown faced yellow; 5th Regiment – brown faced re yellow hunting shirts; Quakers – light blue faced whit Rangers – brown hunting shirts; Light Horse – brow faced white, round hats bound silver, buckstail, yello standard.

For those battalions in 'Continental Service' th following uniform details are known: 1st – brown face green, grey waistcoats, buckskin breeches, buttons wi the inscription '1P.B' and cocked hats; 2nd Battalion blue faced red, red waistcoats, leather breeches, ar buttons with '2.P.B' on them; 3rd Battalion – brown face white, buckskin breeches, buttons with the inscriptic 'No.3', and hats bound white; 4th Battalion – blue face white, white small clothes, hats bound yellow, red lig infantry caps bound black, and white stocks; 5th Battalic – brown faced red, red jackets, buckskin breeches, butto with the inscription '5.P.B', red, brown and whi epaulettes for sergeants; 6th Battalion – blue turned-u red, small round hats.

Maryland

Maryland's Convention organised its forces on 14 Augu 1775 when it voted for the establishment of 40 companic of minutemen and reorganised the militia. In Januar 1776, it abolished the minutemen and established a nin company state regiment, this consisted of two companic of state artillery and seven independent companies – or for each district. The land forces were to have a huntin shirt of colours other than blue. The artillerymen were t receive a new hat, a short coat, waistcoat, breeches and hunting shirt each year. In the case of the independer companies and the Maryland Battalion the cost of clothin was deducted from pay. The uniform of the 2nd Marylan Artillery Company was blue faced red, yellow button hole and a light jacket; the third's was similar but with whit button holes. For details of the 1st Company see Figure Plate E.

Enlisted men of the Maryland Battalion wore huntin shirts, coats, overalls and hats. Officers were clothed i scarlet faced buff. Baltimore Independent Cadets wor coats turned-up with buff, yellow buttons, white stocking and black half boots. In the Independent Companies th hunting shirt was almost universal: in addition the 3r Company wore black uniforms; the shirts of the 4t Company had red cuffs, and the riflemen of this compan were issued capes. In the 5th Company leather caps wer worn.

'Rough' sketch dated 9 February 1776 of a knapsack/haversack adopted for use by Maryland, New Jersey,

Virginia and Pennsylvania forces. (Smithsonian photograph, MdHR 4561, Maryland Hall of Records,

Virginia

Following the expiry of the Militia Law in March 1775, the Convention of Delegates resolved to replace the militia with two regiments of regulars, two frontier independent companies and a battalion of minutemen. These units were recruited from the militia in each of the sixteen provincial districts. Minutemen and regulars who signed up without their own clothing would be furnished, at public expense,

Rifleman, Captain Church's Company, 4th Pennsylvania Battalion, Summer 1776. He wears a short blue double-breasted regimental coat faced white, white waistcoat, drilling breeches and a red cap bound black. (Peter F. Copeland)

with a hunting shirt and a pair of leggings. The number of regular regiments was increased to nine on 1 December 1775, and the Convention of Delegates added hat binding, facing cloth and leggings to the clothing allowance. At this time, a Public Store in Williamsburg was established, which, under William Aylett, Commissary of Supplies was to provide arms, accoutrements and clothing. Throughout the war, the Virginia Public Store clothed the state's land and naval forces, and its Continental regiments, from the profits of tobacco export.

The clothing of the constituent units of the Minute Battalion and the independent companies varied quite markedly. Uniform details were as follows: Fairfax County Independent Company (1774–76) – blue turned-up with buff, plain yellow metal buttons, buff waistcoat and breeches, white stockings. In addition George Washington procured, for this unit, a colour bearing the motto '*Aut Liber aut Nullus*', officers' gorgets and halberds, and shoulder knots for sergeants and corporals; Prince William County Independent Company of Cadets – the unit's colour, officers' sashes and gorgets, and gold shoulder knots for sergeants and corporals were supplied by General Washington; Independent Company of Alexandria (1775) – for this unit Washington provided a pattern of hunting shirt, cap and gaiters; Culpeper County Minute Battalion (1775–76) – the colour for this battalion displayed a coiled rattlesnake in its centre, below it the words 'Don't tread on me', at the sides 'Liberty or Death', and at the top 'The Culpeper Minute Men'. The men wore brown linen hunting shirts dyed green with the inscription in large white letters on the breast, 'Liberty or Death', buckstail for cockades, blue stroud leggings with scarlet garters and horn buttons, leather shoulder belts for tomahawks, and scalping knives; Prince William County Minute Battalion (1775) – blue hunting shirts and red leggings.

Of Virginia's regiments in Continental service the following uniform details are known: 1st – dyed hunting shirts faced scarlet, blue overalls, round hats, black camp colours, racoon rifle pouches and blue kersey watchcoats; 2nd – purple hunting shirts, blue kersey watchcoats and white camp colours; 3rd – dyed hunting shirts and blue leggings; 4th – red faced green, and yellow buttons; 5th – hunting shirts; 6th – short brown oznabrig hunting shirts, colour and cuffs faced with red, drummer's and fifer's shirts were white with brown cuffs (for further detail see Figure 3, Plate C); 7th – black hunting shirts, blue waistcoats, and leather breeches; 8th – brown hunting

shirts and trousers, blue coats, yellow buttons, and buckskin breeches; Light Horse – blue close bodied coats with red cape and cuffs, leather breeches, a pair of pistols and holsters, a tomahawk, a spear and a saddle; Artillery Company – coats of blue faced white.

North Carolina

North Carolina raised two battalions of regulars in 1775, and placed them on the Continental establishment in order to secure support for uniforms from the Continental Congress. On 24 December 1775, the Council of State resolved that in districts where Continental troops were stationed, paymasters would buy cloth to be made into coats, waistcoats and breeches for the two battalions. In addition to the regulars, each of the six regional military districts was required to raise a ten-company battalion of minutemen whose bounty consisted of a uniform that comprised a hunting shirt, leggings or spatterdashes, and black garters.

To provide for its nine Continental regiments, North Carolina's delegates to the Continental Congress informed the Council of Safety on 2 August 1776 that they had appointed James Mease one of the Continental commissaries. Mease was employed to make up cloth short coats, breeches, stockings, shoes and shirts. A later requisition included such items as hats, cartouche boxes, canteens and regimental colours. On 18 October, Mease consigned to the Council of Safety at Halifax: 560 coats mixed faced red, 592 coats drab faced blue, 16 drummers coats in blue faced drab, 608 coats brown faced white, 16 drummers coats white faced brown, 411 coats drab faced red, 476 coats brown faced red, 506 pairs of drilling breeches, and 500 oznabrig shirts. No record has been found of the distribution of this shipment.

South Carolina

South Carolina's militia of 14,000 officers and men was organised into 12 regiments of foot and one of horse. In addition the First Provincial Congress formed volunteer companies and troops of horse. On 4 June 1775, the Provincial Congress authorised the raising of two regiments of foot and one of rangers as regulars on South Carolina's establishment.

Captain Jacob Shubrick, 2nd South Carolina Regiment of the Continental Line, by Henry Benbridge. Probably painted after Shubrick's death at Fort Moultrie in June 1778. He wears a grenadier officer's uniform consisting of a black mitre cap, garters, scabbard, spatterdashes and stock; silver crescent, epaulettes, buttons and sword hilt; blue coat; scarlet lapels, cape, cuffs and lining; white waistcoat, breeches, stockings, and frills. (The Society of the Cincinnati Museum, Anderson House, Washington DC)

The known uniform details of South Carolina's militia are as follows: 1st Regiment (June 1775) – officers' regimentals were blue faced buff, cap and feather, however from 1776 regimentals were to be blue faced red; 2nd Regiment (June 1775) – officers' regimentals blue faced scarlet, cap and feather, and crescent in front bearing the motto 'Liberty', two regimental standards, one red and one blue (see illustration on page 38 for detail of the blue standard); 3rd Regiment (Rangers) (December 1775) – equipped as riflemen, uniforms were of blue faced white, fronted caps inscribed with the motto 'Liberty or Death' were also worn; Edisto Island Volunteers (1775) – blue coat with white cuffs and lapels, white waistcoat and breeches and fan-tail hat; Captain Charles Drayton's Volunteers (1775) – officers in scarlet frock coats, faced with white and silver metal; St Helena Volunteers (1775) – blue coatees faced red, standing collar, white small clothes, black kneebands and gaiters, beaver cap with silver crescent and inscribed with the motto 'Liberty or Death', white plume on the right and black ostrich plume on the left; Regiment of Horse, Provincial Militia (1761–75) – blue coats with yellow buttons and crimson lining, cuffs, lapels and waistcoat; blue breeches, gold laced hat, officers' waistcoats laced, blue saddle cloth and blue fringed holster; Artillery Company of Charleston (1757–76) – blue coatee, crimson lapels and cuffs, gilt buttons, blue waistcoats and breeches; Light Infantry Company of Charleston (1773–75) – scarlet short coats faced black were worn with gold lace for officers and plain lace for soldiers, white waistcoats and breeches, black caps with black feathers and a silver crescent inscribed with the motto '*Pro patria*' completed the uniform.

Georgia

The poorest and least populated of all the provinces, Georgia had to rely on help from the Continental Congress to begin raising a regular regiment. A volunteer company of light infantry and one of grenadiers existed in Savannah, but, like the regulars, no information on uniforms is available.

CONTINENTAL UNIFORMS

On 18 July 1775, the Continental Congress resolved to inform each province that all men entering a military association should come with a good firelock, bayonet, cutting sword or tomahawk, cartridge box with 24 rounds, a powder horn with 2 lbs powder and 2 lbs lead in a bag, and a knapsack.

The procurement of military clothing was assigned to the Continental Quartermaster General at Cambridge, Major Thomas Mifflin, appointed 16 June 1775. Mifflin's appeals of 6 and 11 September to Congress for funds to buy coarse woollens compelled the delegates to debate the neglected issue of clothing the two armies Congress had raised – the Cambridge Army, commanded by Washington, and the Northern Army, campaigning against Canada. On 23 September 1775, Congress voted to form a committee to buy £5,000 worth of woollens, to be placed in the hands of the Quartermaster General. For his trouble, Mifflin received a commission of five per cent of the prime cost and charges attributable to this activity. To supply its Northern Army, on 2 November 1775, Congress ordered Francis Lewis and John Alsop of New York to purchase 3,000 felt hats, 3,000 caps, 3,000 pairs of buckskin breeches, 3,000 waistcoats, 3,000 pairs of shoes, and 300 watchcoats of fearnought or duffel.

Provision of uniforms

As domestic supplies of cloth rapidly dwindled and prices soared, the Continental Congress committee recommended, on 23 December 1775, the importation of 60,000 striped blankets, 120,000 yards of blue and brown broad cloth, 10,000 yards of different coloured broad cloths for facing, and 3,000 yards of duffel. As a result of this report, on 3 January 1776, Congress authorised the Secret Committee to negotiate contracts with merchants, such as Nicholas and John Brown of Rhode Island, to take commercial voyages with the object of importing the above cloth. Among the early results of this effort was the aptly named brig *Happy Return*, which brought over 2,000 yards each of brown and blue cloth into Providence.

Supplementing this commercial activity, the Committee of Secret Correspondence ordered Silas Deane of Connecticut, then representing the 13 colonies in France, to apply for clothing and arms to be paid for by remittances as soon as navigation opened.

It was not until 19 June 1776 that Congress recommended that the rebelling colonies should provide each soldier enlisted from their colonies with a suit of clothes for

the 1777 campaign. This was to include buckskin waistco and breeches, a blanket, a hat or leather cap, two pairs hose, two shirts and two pairs of shoes. Congress wou pay for them and would be reimbursed from soldiers' pa Most of the states had already taken action to clothe th troops, but where necessary they appointed commissar to represent the Continental effort. Many agents, such Samuel Allyne Otis of Boston, Daniel Tillinghast of Rho Island, James Mease of Philadelphia and William Ayle simply served both masters.

Following the creation of a war department in the for of the Continental Board of War and Ordnance, on October 1796 Congress resolved to appoint a Commissa of Clothing for each of the regional armies. Geor Measam, a native of Canada, was appointed to t Northern Army, and James Mease, the Continental age in Philadelphia, was appointed by General Washington 10 February 1777 to the broader position of Cloth General.

In the meantime, General Washington was putting army into some measure of order. Washington's Gene Orders of 14 and 24 July specified the following ra insignia for officers and non-commissioned office commanders-in-chief – a light blue ribbon across t breast between the coat and waistcoat; major generals – purple ribbon; brigadier generals – a pink ribbon; aide de-camp – a green ribbon; field officers – a red or pi cockade; captains – yellow or buff; subalterns – gree sergeants – an epaulette or strip of red cloth sewn on t right shoulder; and for corporals one of green. For all m on duty without uniform, Washington recommended, b did not order, a practical and inexpensive uniform o hunting shirt and long breeches made gaiter fashion. went on to try to convince the governors of Rhode Isla

Right: Georgia four spanish milled dollars certificate, c.1776. The figure in the bottom right hand corner wears a Scottish bonnet with a feather in the front, single breasted jacket, fringed kilt, overalls and moccasins. (Private Collection)

Left: Georgia three dollar certificate, dated 10 September 1777. The figure wears a Kilmarnock bonnet, single breasted jacket, wide kilt, leggings and moccasins. (Smithsonian photograph)

and Connecticut and the Continental Congress to adopt the hunting shirt as the standard American uniform.

Washington's dream of a hunting shirt clad army was shattered by the lack of tow cloth in both Connecticut and Rhode Island. At a meeting of delegates from the Continental Congress held at Cambridge on 20 October, it was agreed that clothing provided by the Continent was to be paid for from the soldiers' wages – 10 shillings per month. Cloth for this purpose was to be dyed brown, and regimental distinctions were made in the facings. On 17 November 1775, Washington ordered the officers commanding the 26 Continental Regiments of Foot to meet at the office of the Quartermaster General at Cambridge to agree uniforms for their regiments.

To make these uniforms, the Quartermaster General could draw on captured British uniforms amounting to 338 scarlet faced pale buff coats of the 22nd Regiment of Foot, 36 scarlet faced buff coats of the 40th Foot, two bales containing 420 yards of blue broad cloth, and four casks and nine bales of cloth and clothing sent by Francis Lewis to John Alsop in Cambridge. These were to be made up into 2,000 blue, brown and green coats and waistcoats, faced in red, blue, pink, green, yellow, white, buff, brown and crimson. The $\frac{6}{4}$ wide cloth would provide $2\frac{1}{2}$ yards to make up a short coat and a belted waistcoat, like those of the Philadelphia *Associators*. Some 2,000 felt hats with white binding were also to be forwarded.

The regimentals drawn by the colonels of the 26 Continental regiments became available for delivery at cost on 5 January 1776. On 20 February, Washington ordered that each regiment was to be furnished with colours that would match the regimental uniform. The suit of colours of each regiment consisted of two standards and four colours for each grand division. The first standard was to be the Union, and the second was to be in the colour of the facings and marked with the number of the regiment and a motto.

Uniforms and colours of the Continental Regiments of Foot

1st Regiment
Officers wore green coats and breeches. The regimental standard featured a tiger enclosed by netting, defended by a hunter in white and armed with a spear, on a crimson field with the motto 'Dominari Nollo'. For details of the uniforms of enlisted men see Figure 2, Plate B.

7th Regiment
Sailor's dress. This regiment's standard had a white field with a black thorn bush and a flesh coloured hand extended to pluck the bush. The standard bore the motto 'He that touches me shall prick his fingers'.

11th Regiment
Men wore brown hunting shirts and coats faced with white. Officers' uniforms had silver lace.

12th Regiment
Blue coats faced buff.

13th Regiment
Regimental standard was light buff, with a pine tree and a field of Indian corn. The standard depicted two officers in regimental uniform, one wounded in the breast with blood

streaming from the wound pointing to several children under the tree, with the motto 'For posterity I bleed'.

15th Regiment
At Trenton, on 25 December 1776, Fife Major Isaac Greenwood lost his pack containing a suit of blue turned-up with white, and silver laced; Captain Ebenezer Sullivan, when taken prisoner on 20 May 1776, lost his blue coat faced white with two gold epaulettes, white jacket and breeches, gold laced hat, and blue surtout coat with green velvet collar.

16th Regiment
Deserter reports indicate uniforms of green and a standard of red on a white field.

17th Regiment
Regimental coats had black lapels, these were made for Lieutenant Jabez Fitch on 14 February 1776.

18th Regiment
A deserter had a cloth coloured coat faced buff. The uniform of the regiment was a narrow brimmed felt hat bound white. The regimental standard was buff.

22nd Regiment
Lieutenant Roger Hooker's inventory of personal possessions included a scarlet faced buff coat with a gold

epaulette, a blue coat faced with red, a red duffel watchcoat, a red and a white pair of breeches, two white, one blue and one red vest, two pairs of black silk knee garters, two beaver hats, one which was trimmed with gold, four white shirts, one white goat skin haversack, a cartouche box and a bayonet belt.

24th Regiment
A deserter report describes a man in a Continental coat and jacket (July). The regimental standard was buff with a red field, white thorn bush with a flesh coloured hand extended to pluck it, and the motto: 'He that touches me shall prick his fingers'.

25th Regiment
One blue and buff coat issued at Albany on 20 September 1776; the regiment was credited with 601 uniform coats and 270 waistcoats.

26th Regiment
Uniforms consisted of a brown coat, blue jacket and white breeches, for further details see Figure 1, Plate B. For detail of regimental mitre caps see the pictures on pages 7 and 44. The unit's standard was straw coloured.

Regiment of Artillery (Knox's)
According to the papers of Henry Knox and the orderly book of Captain Ezra Badlam, the regiment had blue coats, red two inch wide lapels, cape and cuffs, white lining, gold buttons, white waistcoats, buff leather breeches, blue stockings, black half-gaiters, and black hats with black cockade and gilt buttons; drummers' and fifers' coats were scarlet faced blue.

Major Jeremiah Dugan's Canadian Rangers
Officers received blue and red cloth, coarse linen, buttons and thread to make a coat, waistcoat and breeches, and a pair of moccasins. Enlisted men received blanket coats, spotted swanskin waistcoats, cloth breeches, russia sheeting shirts, ratteen leggings, mittens, shoes and milled caps.

Grenadier mitre cap, 26th Continental Infantry Regiment, 1776. Full front view. This example is believed to have been worn by Corporal Ansel Pope, Captain Thomas Mighill's Company. The front of the cap is 12 inches high, 10½ inches wide at the base and covered with red wool. Embroidered in white thread on the front is the monogram 'GW' and a sunburst. The cap itself is edged in white herringbone tape. The 4 inch high flap is in the facing colour of straw yellow, with gold edging. (Collections of the Division of Armed Forces History, National Museum of American History, Smithsonian Institution)

Uniforms and specifications 1777–78

When Congress established a new Continental Army of 88 battalions of Line infantry, five regiments of artillery, one of artillery artificers, 16 additional regiments not assigned to any state, five regiments raised in 1776 for the war (1st and 2nd Canadians, German Battalion, Warner's Green Mountain Boys, the Maryland and Virginia Rifle Regiments), four regiments of light dragoons and a squadron of Provost Guards, the clothing of these troops became the conflicting objective of Congress, the individual states and Washington's subordinate commanders. In this process, Washington's role was that of a referee.

Continental clothing depots were established either in camp with the armies or in convenient locations. Before the fall of Philadelphia, Congress instructed Mease to buy up all available supplies of cloth, caps and hats in Philadelphia. After the capture of Philadelphia, York and Lancaster served as the locations for Continental clothing stores in Pennsylvania.

To serve the Northern Army, clothing stores were established first in Albany and then, in 1777, in Fishkill and Peekskill, New York. Assisting Mease were clerks, storekeepers and a deputy in each state. Clothing was issued direct to non-commissioned officers, and appropriate amounts were deducted from soldiers' pay.

Mease's direct responsibilities included the line, cavalry, artillery and additional regiments within his reach,

Etching, 'The Death of Warren' frontispiece from Brackenridge, The Battle of Bunkers-Hill (Philadelphia, 1776). This contemporaneous illustration is not based on any known British or European work; therefore, it may be considered a faithful depiction of the military dress worn by defenders of the famous hill. Note the dragoon sleeve and the narrow cape and lapels on the coat of the kneeling figure. Three background figures have short hunting shirts with fringed capes, flopped hats turned-up, and leggings or overalls worn into the shoes. (Library of Congress)

Massachusetts Provincial Congress coat, reconstructed by Peter F. Copeland. Made by various Massachusetts townships in response to the call of the Provincial Congress for uniforms for the troops raised by the colony. It had no lapels and was faced with the material of the coat, The number of the regiment was displayed on the pewter buttons. Made of homespun cloth, these coats were used extensively by New England forces during 1776.

altered by removing the white lapels from the 47th's coats and using them as cuffs and capes on those of the other two. Hoping to issue these to Colonel William Grayson's Additional Regiment of Foot from Virginia, Mease found that Grayson had already settled on 400 blue faced red coats. The Commander-in-Chief's Guard was to have facings of buff, but with this colour in short supply, Mease substituted yellow.

In the Northern Department, on 5 September, George Measam, from Albany, informed General Gates of the arrival from Boston of a 'fine' parcel of 581 blue and red uniforms, and from James Mease in Philadelphia of 386 brown faced red coats, 118 brown faced white, 150 brown faced green, 136 blue faced red, 60 drab faced red, 96 drab faced green and 20 drummers' and fifers' coats of green faced blue. On 5 October, Measam received from Massachusetts 600 coats blue faced white, 104 brown faced white, 470 brown linen shirts, as well as various other items of clothing. While the above totals 1,847 coats, an account for the Northern Army in the US National Archives enumerates 3,497 coats issued during 1777.

Notwithstanding this effort, complaints of lack of clothing kept coming to General Washington, who blamed much of the shortfall on individual officers, accusing them of neglecting their men, inflating their requirements, and engaging in other time-honoured practices.

Mease, in a letter dated 4 December 1777 to Washington, asked to be relieved of his duties owing to ill-health, but promised to fulfil his responsibilities until a successor was named.

Accounting to the Board of War Committee on Clothing, Mease reported on all issues, including those to the Northern Army, but excluding South Carolina and Georgia which did not file clothing returns. On 1 January 1778 issues stood at: 22,586 coats, 21,880 waistcoats, 22,237 pairs of breeches, 53,002 shirts, 53,658 pairs of shoes, 44,818 pairs of stockings, 10,451 hats, 11,308 blankets, 6,087 hunting shirts, 14,936 pairs of overalls, 1,276 pairs of mitts, 514 pairs of boots, 1,162 milled caps and 337 gaiters and garters. To measure the adequacy of this distribution against requirements, exclusive of the artillery, the strength of Washington's army in December 1777 was 10,276 rank and file present and fit for duty out of a total 25,985.

During 1777, Washington issued no order specifying a uniform colour or pattern for the Continental Army, but on 28 December 1777, he accepted a uniform pattern recommended by the Marquis de Lafayette for the 1778 issues. Washington described it as a 'waistcoat, in the French fashion', with large lapels turned back in fair weather and buttoned over the breast in cold. It had a high standing $1\frac{1}{2}$ inch collar and three inch cuffs of a different

but not the Continental service departments such as the Quartermaster General, the Hospital, and the Commissary General of Military Stores, all of which took care of their own personnel.

Mease first made use of captured British clothing. Writing to Washington on 12 May 1777, he proposed issuing to Colonel John Moylan's 4th Continental Light Dragoons some 250 scarlet faced blue coats of the 8th and 21st Foot. For the outcome of this expedient move, see Figure 1, Plate D. The remaining 450 coats of these two regiments were shortened and their body linings removed. Coats belonging to the 47th, 53rd and 62nd Foot were

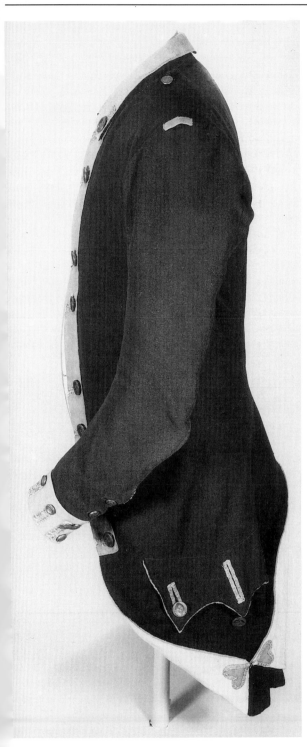

colour; these varied to distinguish regiments. Lafayette's round hat had a three inch brim turned up on one side and adorned with a small feather, an under jacket without a pocket or belt, and either overalls or breeches and stockings. Rather than wear stockings, he recommended the soldiers grease the inside of their shoes and cover the shoes with half gaiters.

Imported Uniforms 1777–78

The Continental Congress first ordered imported ready-made uniforms when on 17 February 1777 the Secret Committee instructed the Continental Commissioners at Paris to obtain 40,000 uniforms in green, blue and brown, with facings. The coats and waistcoats were to be short skirted and made to suit men of stouter stature than those of France. Orders were for batches of 10,000 or less. The uniforms were either brown or blue and had red facings and white metal buttons. They were to include white cloth waistcoats and breeches. A contract of 6 August 1777 for 5,000 coats specifies red linings as well as facings and collars. The other contracts call for white linings.

Uniforms that did reach the Continental Clothier were highly praised by George Measam: they were good quality

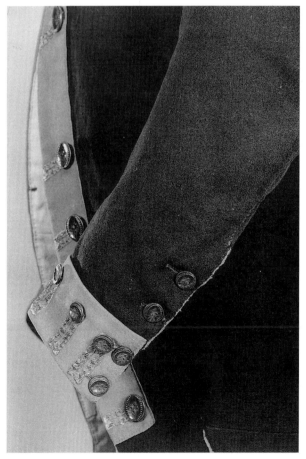

egimental coat of ‚olonel Peter Gansevoort, ‚rd New York Regiment of ‚he Continental Line, ‚777–79. The skirts are ‚ooked back revealing red ‚earts with silver lace and ‚e ½ inch wide red welt edging on the pocket. Shoulder strap retainers were red, 2 inches long and ½ inch wide. Note the narrow red welt marks on the cuffs. (Smithsonian Institution)

cloth, lined with white serges, and had white waistcoats and breeches. The breeches were made for knee-buckles, which were not supplied, the coats were well cut, being large and warm with the lapels made to button over the breast and belly, with plain white buttons and slash sleeves made to button underneath. The coats and waistcoats were lined with white serge and the breeches with strong brown linen. Stockings were lead coloured.

No uniforms for non-commissioned officers or drummers and fifers were received in these consignments. As of 23 July 1778 Mease reported the arrival of the following imported clothing: 22,596 coats, 23,074 waistcoats, 23,074 pairs of breeches, 1276 suits in the brig *Three Brothers*, 12,098 shoes, 16,130 stockings and 4,986 blankets. This clothing was to be distributed to the Continental Infantry which in December 1778 returned 17,343 rank and file fit for duty.

Allocation of these uniforms was determined by a lottery held in two drawings by Washington's aides-de-camp. On 28 October 1778, they drew lots to determine which colour – brown or blue – went to which state line.

The results of the first draw were: blue for North Carolina, Maryland, New Jersey and New York; and brown for Virginia, Delaware, Pennsylvania, Massachusetts, New Hampshire and Hazen's Regiment. States that drew brown coats participated in a second lottery for access to any remaining undistributed blue coats. A record of 4,232 brown and blue coats, and the same number of white waistcoats and pairs of breeches, distributed to Gate's Division between 4 and 11 November 1778, confirms the lottery's allocations.

In April 1778, the Continental Board of War prepared an estimate for 100,000 uniforms to be imported for the campaign of 1779. The suits were to be sized as the French uniforms, except that the skirts of the coat were not to reach below half-way down the thigh. When made up, the clothing was to have extra cloth at the seams, to enable it to be altered if too small, and sleeves wide enough to give the soldier the free use of his arms. The coat was to button as far as the waistband, and the buttons were to be of block tin or brass, solid cast, with a strong eye or shank. Each button bore the inscription 'USA' in Roman letters. The linings.

Cartouche of 'A Map of that part of Pensylvania [sic] now the Principle seat of War in America wherein may be seen the Situation of Philadelphia, Red Bank, Mud Island, & Germantown...'. Etching 1777. The officer represents the American forces and shows a pattern uniform that resembles that used pre-1775. (Library of Congress)

except for those of the Artillery, were to be the same colour as the facings, and the sergeants' clothes were to be of a better quality.

Infantry uniforms were to be blue faced white, blue faced scarlet, white faced blue, blue faced yellow and green faced white. The drummers' and fifers' uniforms were reversed, and 1,200 of the soldiers' coats were to be furnished with knots for corporals. For light dragoons, complete suits, including cloaks, were to be of green faced white, blue faced white, white faced blue and blue faced yellow, with trumpeters' coat colours reversed. Corporals' knots were to be fixed to 120 privates' coats in each group. Plain caps with green, black, red and white horsehair crests were ordered in proportion to the suits. Material for officers' uniforms, following the same colour schemes as those of the infantry, light dragoons and artillery were also estimated. Officers' buttons were to be white and yellow with the letters 'USA' stamped on them. The officers were to have white worsted hose, fine linen for shirts and cambric stocks. For enlisted men, the estimate specified hats laced with white bindings and feathers of the Kevehuller cock, black stocks, brass shirt-sleeve buttons and stock buckles.

Continental Artillery

Descriptions of deserters, tailoring orders of Brigadier General Henry Knox and comments on orders for clothing for the Artillery by Messrs Otis and Andrews reveal the following uniform details: black coats lapelled with red, plain yellow buttons, white waistcoats, breeches and stockings, black garters, cocked hats, hair cockades and white tassels. The above details are supported by clothing records of the 2nd and 3rd regiments.

The first consolidated delivery of clothing to all four regiments was in October 1778. Officers received regimental coats and brown breeches. For non-commissioned officers and drummers, Knox requested two-inch wide white leather sword belts to wear over the shoulder. Hats for the whole brigade were to be cocked without being cut, and ornamented with a piece of bearskin. Drummers' and fifers' hats were to be cut round and turned-up on one side. An invoice in the National Archives, prepared by the Board of War on 30 April 1778 for clothing to be imported from France, details the Artillery clothing for the campaign of 1779 as: suits of black faced with scarlet, with yellow trimmings and lined in white. Coats for corporals, gunners and bombardiers were to have knots, while those of the drums and fifes were to be scarlet faced with black.

In April and May 1778, Harrison's 1st Continental Artillery Regiment received from the Virginia Public Store: 221 blue coats with red lapels, 74 striped waistcoats and pairs of breeches and 30 red jackets and pairs of

Colonel Henry Jackson of Jackson's Additional Continental Regiment of Foot, after an original in the Essex Institute of Salem, Massachusetts, by an unknown artist. Painted while Jackson's regiment was stationed at Dorchester Heights in 1777, he wears blue faced buff, buff waistcoat and breeches, black cocked hat and white ruffles. (Peter F. Copeland)

breeches. Two Maryland companies, that joined the 1st Regiment in July, were also uniformed in blue faced scarlet. And in October 1778, the regiment received 142 yards of black cloth from the Virginia clothier at camp.

The 4th Continental Artillery Regiment was a Pennsylvania state regiment until transferred to the Continental Army by an act of the General Assembly of 18 June 1777. For details of its uniforms, see the Pennsylvania section below.

Benjamin Flower's Regiment of Artillery and Artificers does not appear to have been uniformed during this period.

Continental Light Dragoons

On 7 March 1778, Major General Horatio Gates, President of the Board of War, informed the governors of the states that the minimum needed to equip a horseman for the field was: a straight bladed sword, three feet long, open guarded and with a leather scabbard; a pair of pistols and holsters; a sword belt; a carbine belt with a running swivel; a cartridge box to buckle round the waist and 12 tin pipes for the cartridges; a helmet of jacked leather, guarded by

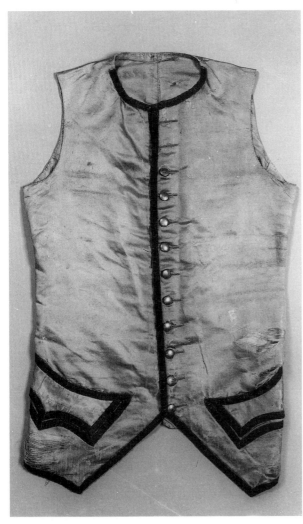

Waistcoat of Major General Adam Stephen. White silk front and back, silver lace and buttons. Stephen, a veteran of the French and Indian War, commanded the 4th Virginia Regiment of the Continental Line until promoted to brigadier general on 4 September 1776. He was promoted once more, this time to major general, on 19 February 1777, Stephen was 'dismissed [from] the service' for drunkenness at Germantown. (Collections of the Division of Armed Forces History, National Museum of American History, Smithsonian Institution)

several rows of small chains with iron or steel hoops, or a hat with a metal scull piece inside the crown; a saddle, saddle cloth, breast plate, crupper, saddle straps and pad; saddle bags; a double-reined bridle with curb and snaffle bit, and a halter; a cloak sufficient to cover all the arms and accoutrements; and a pair of boots and spurs.

1st Light Dragoons
On 13 April 1777, Colonel Theodrick Bland issued a complete regimental order that included: brown coats with a green interrupted lapel, a standing collar and angular cuff, gold buttons cast with a horse and the number '1', and button holes; green vests without skirts; buff breeches; (for trumpeters see Figure 3 Plate D); for farriers and saddlers plain brown coats with green lapels, white sword belts and slings, leather caps with perpendicular fronts, green turbans with yellow tassels, and plain leather holster caps marked with the number '1'. Cloth for the regimentals, which was used until 1780, was obtained from the Virginia Public Store and the helmets and boots came from Baltimore.

2nd Light Dragoons
Other than their own clothes and horse equipment supplied by Connecticut, and a few hunting shirts provided by the Continental Clothier General, the 2nd had no uniform in 1777. When in 1778 Lieutenant Colonel Blackden went to New England to contract for boots, breeches and coats, all the regiment could boast of was 140 heavy horsemen's swords with steel scabbards taken from General Burgoyne. A fragment bill signed by Samuel Blackden in the National Archives is for brass for helmets.

3rd Light Dragoons
Some of the Virginia-recruited troops of this regiment joined wearing Virginia Light Horse uniforms. By mid September 1777, the Clothier General had issued 246 coats, 81 vests, 47 pairs of breeches and eight pairs of boots to the regiment. However, a pattern uniform seems only to have been adopted in April 1778 when Colonel George Baylor purchased from the Virginia Public Store: 176 yards of white cloth, $77\frac{1}{4}$ yards of blue and other cloths, and 48 black feathers for the officers. On 27 September 1778 Captain Robert Smith was sent to Otis and Andrews in Boston to obtain regimental uniforms. Otis and Andrews had no difficulty making cloaks for the regiment, but shortage of white cloth meant that the uniforms were not delivered until 1779.

4th Light Dragoons
The use of captured British clothing by this regiment is discussed earlier in this chapter. For further detail see Figure 1, Plate D.

North Carolina Light Horse
Raised in North Carolina for Continental service, this troop was uniformed by the Clothier General with 70 coats, 70 waistcoats, 70 pairs of breeches, 70 hunting shirts, 70 pairs of shoes and 59 pairs of boots. While serving Fort Pitt in 1778, the troop also received blue and red cloth from the store keeper of the Western Department.

Continental Legionary Corps

Armand's Corps

On 17 May 1778, the Continental Board of War authorised Colonel Armand, Marquis de la Rouerie – commander of the independent corps of Major Ottendorf, to form a corps of Free and Independent Chasseurs. After examining the needs of his new corps, Armand wrote to Lieutenant Colonel Alexander Hamilton on 5 November 1778 requesting 100 knapsacks, 141 pairs of woollen breeches, 141 worsted caps, 112 pairs of long gaiters, 24 cloaks and 24 linen wraps from the store at Fishkill.

Lee's Legion

Formed as a detachment from the 1st Continental Light Dragoons, Lee's Legion did not possess a distinct uniform until July 1778 when Major Henry Lee purchased 305 yards of buff cloth, 130 yards of green cloth and 156 pairs of yarn hose from the Virginia Public Store.

Pulaski's Legion

A clear picture of the uniforms worn by men of Pulaski's Legion in 1778 can be constructed from a general return of clothing and accoutrements preserved in the New York Historical Society, (see Figure 3, Plate H). During 1778, the Legion received 619 coats, 262 leather jackets, 353 pairs of leather breeches, 222 linen jackets, 85 hunting shirts, 533 caps, 374 pairs of boots, 156 boot buckles, 154 great coats, 350 pairs of gaiters, 250 gaiter tops, 348 leather cockades, 400 stars, 400 feathers, and 234 fur skins. Some 1,835 yards of blue, red, grey, white and other cloth were used to make uniforms for riflemen, dragoons and infantry. Musicians had red coats and trumpeters' coats were bound with silver.

Additional Continental Regiments of Foot

Sixteen regiments were raised regionally but not adopted by any state, so their clothing had to come from the common pool of Continental stores or commanders had to find alternative sources.

*Armaments of the American Rebels. **Pen** sketch with hand colouring, $11\frac{1}{2}$ by $16\frac{1}{4}$ inches. The artist Charles Blaskowitz was the map maker for Major General Howe. Figure 'A' represents a floating battery or gondola built at Cambridge 'by the Rebels' in October 1775. Note the tree displayed on the colour. 'C', 'D' and 'E' are pole arms '. . . in Use in the Rebel Army'. (Library of Congress)*

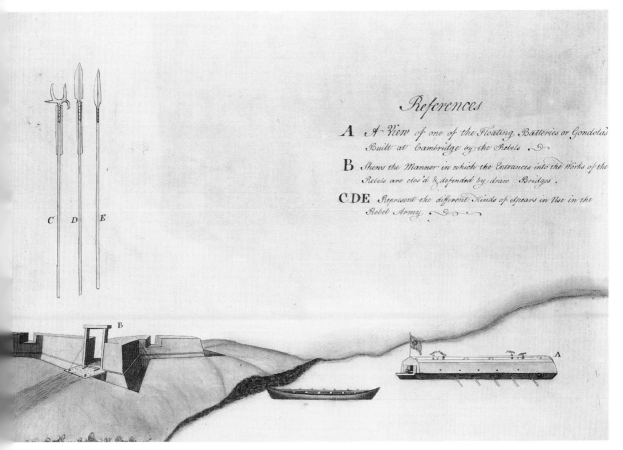

Committee of Safety musket. (Collections of the Division of Armed Forces History, National Museum of American History, Smithsonian Institution)

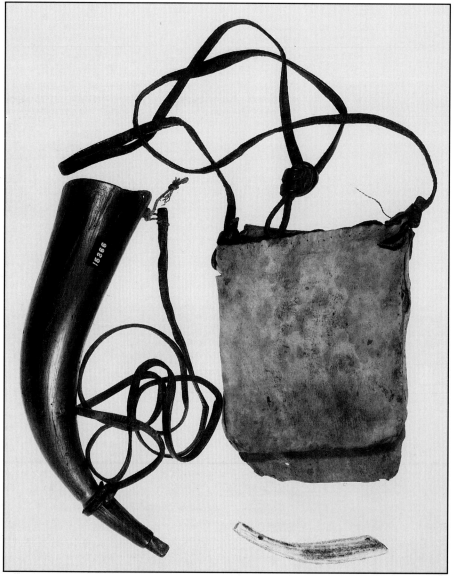

Powder horn, bullet pouch and powder measurer carried by Captain William Walton, 1st North Carolina Regiment of the Continental Line. (Collections of the Division of Armed Forces History, National Museum of American History, Smithsonian Institution)

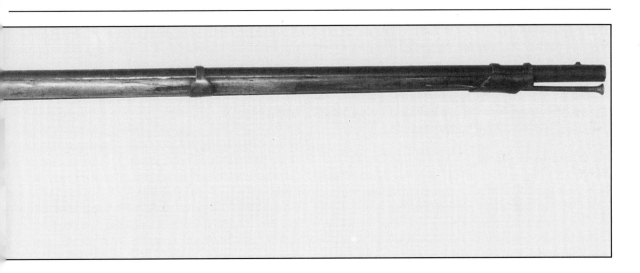

David Forman's

Deserter descriptions and an eye-witness account of the Battle of Germantown describe red coats faced buff, a white jacket, buff breeches and pewter buttons marked '31'.

Nathaniel Gist's

Deserter descriptions specify brown turned-up green, white shirts and brown yarn stockings.

William Grayson's

Blue turned-up with red, red shalloon lined shoulder straps and button holes; on 10 June 1778, the regiment received coats for 180 privates, 29 sergeants and eight drummers from Virginia sources.

Thomas Hartley's

1777: blue coats with white collars, white jackets and buckskin breeches; 1778: blue faced yellow and caps. For further detail see Figure 1, Plate F.

David Henley's

During 1777, 165 soldiers each signed receipt rolls for a hat, coat, waistcoat, shirt, pair of breeches, stock, two pairs of stockings and two pairs of shoes. Deserter descriptions indicate blue regimentals. On 13 October 1778, General Sullivan ordered Henley's, Lee's and Jackson's regiments to be clothed in blue and buff.

Henry Jackson's

This unit's uniform of blue and buff, lined white, white waistcoat and breeches and large hats with white binding was obtained in Boston by Colonel Jackson. For further detail see Figure 2, Plate F.

William R. Lee's

From deserter descriptions it seems that this unit's 1777 uniform included a blue regimental coat faced white.

Oliver Spencer's

By 23 September 1777, the Clothier General had issued the regiment 300 coats, 300 vests, 300 pairs of breeches, 100 pairs of shoes, 110 pairs of hose, 80 shirts, 70 hats or caps, 100 hunting shirts and 165 pairs of overalls.

Seth Warner's

At Albany the regiment received 186 coats, 205 waistcoats, 1,223 pairs of breeches, 65 woollen overalls, 624 shirts, 171 pairs of stockings, 61 hats or caps, 101 hunting shirts, 110 pairs of trousers and 150 blankets.

Samuel Blatchley Webb's

On 18 January 1777, Washington ordered Webb to appropriate captured scarlet clothing sufficient for one regiment. For detail see Figure 3, Plate F.

The uniforms of the regiments of William Malcolm, John Patton, Moses Rawling, Henry Sherburne, Oliver Spencer, Charles Mynn Thruston and Seth Warner are unknown for this period.

Commander-in-Chief's Guard

On 1 January 1778, the Clothier General issued: 90 coats, jackets, pairs of breeches and hats; 94 shirts; 91 pairs of shoes; 111 pairs of stockings; 9 blankets; 1 pair of boots; 180 gaiters or garters; and 90 cockades. Washington expressed a preference for blue and buff, and a miniature portrait of the Guard Commander, Major Caleb Gibbs, shows this combination; in June 1778, 150 suits were reserved for the Guard.

German Battalion

The company book of Captain Philip Graybill's Maryland company in the Maryland Historical Society shows linen hunting shirts for each man. In 1778 a Jacob Smith was wanted for impersonating an officer of the battalion. He was seen wearing a blue coat turned-up with red, a buff jacket and breeches, and blue stockings.

1st Canadian Regiment

In 1777, the regiment received, from the Albany Public Store, 119 pairs of breeches, 62 swanskin jackets, 62 check shirts and 3 blue coats; the Massachusetts Historical Society has clothing returns from 1778 that show caps, shoes, mittens, jackets with sleeves, overalls and coats for some companies.

2nd Canadian Regiment

The men of this regiment wore brown coats with white cuffs and buttons. Waistcoats and breeches were white, black caps were also worn. For further detail see Figure 1, Plate H.

Marechausee Corps

On 14 November 1777, Captain Bartholomew von Heer proposed a Provost corps of 63 men with regimentals of green, or blue coats with black facings; when Congress established this corps on 27 May 1778, Washington wrote to Nathanael Greene, then Continental Quartermaster General, stating that they were to be armed and accoutred as light dragoons.

Invalid Corps

On 23 September 1777, they received from the Clothier General 86 coats, 99 vests, 30 pairs of breeches, 141 pairs of shoes, 107 pairs of hose, 144 shirts, 49 hats or caps and 98 pairs of overalls; in April 1778, Colonel Lewis Nicola, Commandant of the Regiment of Invalids, informed General Washington to be on the lookout for an Invalid wearing a British uniform of a red coat faced buff or white with buttons bearing the number 26. A deserter from the Boston detachment was advertised on 18 January 1779 as wearing a regimental coat of brown faced with red.

Light Corps

On 4 November 1778, Major Thomas Posey's Corps received 80 brown faced red suits, white waistcoats and breeches and grey hose from the Clothier General.

General Staff and Aides-de-Camp

No uniform regulation or details of dress of army staff were published during this period, but personal tailoring bills, correspondence with family members and portraits of general officers and their aides-de-camp indicate that blue faced buff, yellow buttons, gilt epaulettes and buff waistcoats and breeches were the prevalent fashion.

General Washington's uniform of 1776–77 is illustrated in a portrait by Charles Willson Peale. It shows Washington in what was to become his identifying

Hanger and scabbard carried by Brigadier General Richard Montgomery, killed in the assault on Quebec, 31 December 1775.

(Collections of the Division of Armed Forces History, National Museum of American History, Smithsonian Institution)

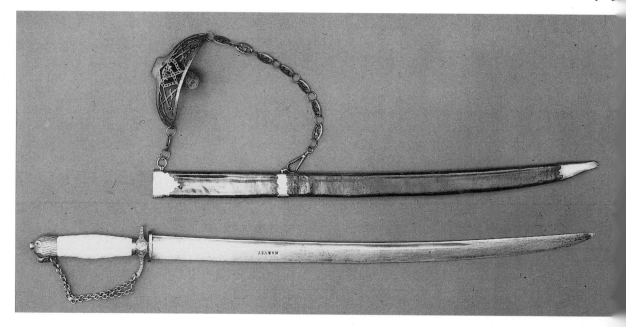

1: Private, Lower Regt. of New Castle, Delaware Militia, 1775-76
2: Grenadier, Captain John Lasher's New York City Grenadier Co., 1775-76
3: Captain Benedict Arnold, Governor's 2nd Co. of Guards, 1775
4: Colonel John Cadwalader, 3rd Bn. Philadelphia Associators, 1775-76

A

1: Grenadier, 26th Continental Regt. of Foot, 1776
2: Rifleman, 1st Continental Regt. of Foot, 1776
3: Chaplain William Emerson, 2nd Continental Regt. of Foot, 1776

1: Corporal, 3rd New Jersey Bn., 1776
2: Captain, Light Infantry Co., 2nd S.C. Regt., 1776-78
3: Corporal, 6th Virginia Regt., 1776-77

C

1: Trooper, 4th Continental Light Dragoons, 1777-78
2: Capt. Samual Chandler, 11th Connecticut Militia Regt., Light Horse Co., 1776-77
3: Trumpeter, 1st Continental Light Dragoons

1: Matross, 1st Co. of Maryland Artillery, 1776
2: Captain, Georgia Artillery, 1778
3: Gunner, 4th S.C. Regt., Artillery, 1775-78

1: Private, Thomas Hartley's Additional Continental Regt. of Foot, 1777
2: Private, Henry Jackson's Additional Continental Regt. of Foot, 1777
3: Ensign, Samuel Blatchley Webb's Additional Continental Regt. of Foot, 1777

1: Private, 4th New York Regt. of the Continental Line, 1778
2: Fifer, 1st New Hampshire Regt. of the Continental Line, 1778
3: Private, 10th North Carolina Regt. of the Continental Line, 1778

1: Private, Light Infantry Co., 2nd Canadian Regt., 1777-78
2: Private, 2nd Rhode Island State Regt., 1777-78
3: Dragoon, Pulaski's Legion, 1778

iform, possibly made for him by Richard Peacock in
nuary 1776. Washington's accounts in the Washington
pers at the Library of Congress indicate that a coat was
ade for him on 28 April 1777. In March 1778, George
ibson, a quartermaster at Lancaster, sent him two pieces
blue and buff cloth of 20 yards each. At General
ashington's order, in November 1778, Otis and Andrews
ade a blue drab surtout coat with blue covered buttons.

From their personal papers, it is evident that Horatio
ates and Nathanael Greene, as general officers, also
lopted the blue and buff uniform with buff waistcoat and
eeches.

Continental Service Departments

ngineers
n 16 July 1776 at Ticonderoga, Colonel Jeduthin
ldwin reported the loss of a blue coat and 'jackoat' full
immed with narrow gold lace, a hat, a pair of silver shoes
d knee buckles.

uartermaster General's Department
January 1778, enlistment advertisements from the
uartermaster General's Department for waggoners and
ivers stipulate that those signing on for three years or the
iration would receive annually a suit of clothing, a great
at and a pair of boots. Clothing forwarded in December
'78 by Colonel Jacob Weiss to Colonel Udney Hay,
eputy Quartermaster General, for Quartermaster Arti-
ers consisted of fully lined brown cloth coats, leather
eeches, yarn stockings, shoes, white linen shirts and
riped Indian blankets.

orps of Waggoners
olonel Henry Luterloch recommended to Washington in
ecember 1777, that the Waggoners should wear a plate or
dge on their breasts in order to identify the department
ey worked in.

STATE UNIFORMS 1777–78

hile each state had the responsibility for clothing their
vn regular corps and, in some cases militia, due to failures
Continental Clothing departments, they also undertook
supply their quota of Continental troops.

*vord and scabbard
rried by Brigadier
eneral Daniel
oberdeau, Pennsylvania
ssociators. (Collections of*

*the Division of Armed
Forces History, Museum of
American History,
Smithsonian Institution)*

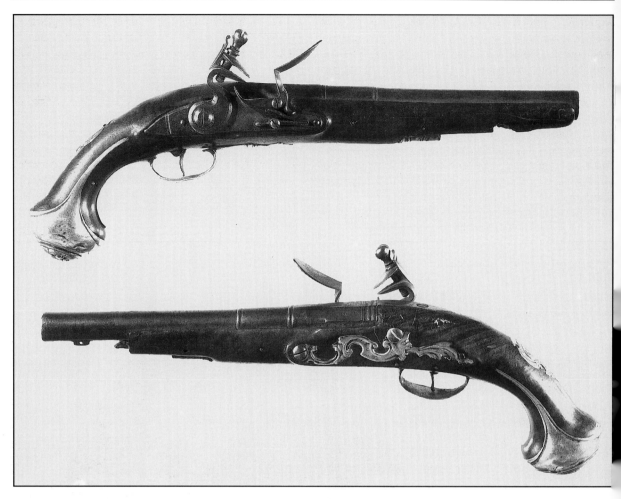

Pair of flintlock pistols owned by Major General Charles Lee. (Collections of the Division of Armed Forces History, Museum of American History, Smithsonian Institution)

Connecticut

On 7 February 1777, Governor Trumbull wrote to General Washington that British clothing of scarlet and buff and scarlet and blue being held in Dartmouth could be of great use to the Connecticut Line. Acting on Washington's approval, on 15 February 1777, the Council of Safety voted that Colonel Jedediah Huntington's 1st Regiment should have the red coats.

For the period 1777–78, the Connecticut Line exemplified the effort required to dress the troops of a given state. On 28 February, Andrew Huntington, a deputy purchaser of clothing, advertised for home-made blue, brown or red cloth for coats, white flannel for waistcoats and breeches, and white yarn for stockings. On 12 September 1777, the Governor and Council of Safety resolved that each town in the state was to donate a shirt, a hunting frock, a pair of woollen overalls, one or two pairs of stockings and a pair of shoes for each soldier in the army belonging to that town.

For the next campaign, the Governor and Council of Safety resolved, on 10 December 1777, to apply to Samuel A. Otis and Benjamin Andrews, the Continental purchasing commissaries at Boston, for delivery of cloth with trimmings sufficient for 4,000 men. The resultant regimental uniforms of 1778 were as follows: 1st Regiment – red faced white, white waistcoat and breeches, small round hats, drummers and fifers wore grey-brown faced light brown, and white small clothes, officers had silver epaulettes and hat cords; 2nd Regiment – dark brown faced white, brown vests and breeches, and hats turned-up on one side, drummers and fifers wore green faced brown; 3rd Regiment – light brown faced red, red or green lining, green waistcoat and breeches and yellow buttons; 4th Regiment – brown faced red, light brown small clothes and yellow binding on hats; 5th Regiment – blue turned-up with scarlet, green vests and breeches, drummers and fifers wore yellow faced brown; 6th Regiment – blue faced white, lined white, white small clothes, and leather caps; 7th

Regiment – miniature of Lt. Augustine Taylor, by John Ramage, unlocated: scarlet coat, white facings and waistcoat, and rose red sash; 8th Regiment – in 1777 uniforms were blue faced scarlet, in 1778 they were scarlet and white.

Rhode Island

On 21 January 1777, the Rhode Island Council of War resolved that Daniel Tillinghast should collect cloth and trimmings for 1,000 coats and pairs of breeches. Tillinghast contracted with various local tailors to make up the cloth, and in April, John Reynolds was empowered to go beyond the state in search of additional cloth.

When, in late August 1777, these efforts to purchase and make clothing did not meet expectations, the 1st Rhode Island Continental Regiment mutinied in late August 1777. Some relief for the two Continental battalions came on 14 January 1778, with the dispatch of eight cases and one cask of clothing to the Rhode Island Brigade at Valley Forge.

When raised in December 1776, the men who enlisted for the State Brigade of two foot and one artillery regiments did not receive clothing, but those who needed uniforms could buy them from the regimental quartermaster. Later, on 19 December 1777, on authorising the re-enlisting of the State Brigade, the General Assembly

Cap worn by the Newport Light Infantry Company, Newport, Rhode Island, 1774–1776. Nothing is known of the uniform of the Company; however, the cap has a $10\frac{3}{16}$ inch high front plate still bearing the royal cypher in silver. On a light blue oval, the female figure America, robed in white and red, stands over broken chains and holds a staff topped by a liberty cap. The belt and scroll with the name of the Company are painted gold. Collections of the Division of Armed Forces History, National Museum of American History, Smithsonian Institution)

stipulated that in addition to a bounty payment, each man would receive a hat, a uniform coat, two waistcoats, two pairs of breeches, three shirts, three pairs of stockings, two pairs of shoes, a hunting shirt and a pair of overalls.

Known uniform details are as follows: 2nd Rhode Island Regiment – deserters from the regiment in 1777 wore brown regimental coats faced with red, brown breeches and black sleeved jackets; 1st Rhode Island State Regiment – a deserter advertised on 13 December 1777 wore a blue coat faced with yellow; 2nd Rhode Island State Regiment – for detail see Figure 2, Plate H; Rhode Island State Artillery Regiment – blue faced red, leather breeches, white waistcoats; drummers in blue coats trimmed with blue and white saddle lace.

Massachusetts

On 10 January 1777, the Massachusetts Council resolved to issue a warrant on the Treasury for four thousand pounds to form a Committee for Clothing. On 17 January,

the Massachusetts Board of War resolved to import from the French merchants Messrs Pliarne, Penet and Company cloth of chocolate, pompadour, claret, berry and blue, with yellow, green, red, buff and white for facings and if these were not available, white cloth with blue facings. By 31 January, the Northern Army was richer by 870 suits of clothing, 95 coats, 171 jackets, 134 overalls, 35 shirts and 457 pairs of hose. An additional 2,300 suits were dispatched by the Continental Agents for the Northern Army to Bennington on 14 February 1777. During that month, the Massachusetts Board of War ordered from Messrs Jacques Gruel and Company 40,000 four-point blankets, 70,000 yards of wool for clothing 20,000 men, 132,000 yards of coarse linen for soldiers' shirts, 20,000 coarse soldiers' hats, 3,000 pieces of ravens duck for tents, 40,000 pairs of shoes fit for soldiers, 40,000 white stockings and 60,000 yards of brown russia drilling for waistcoats and breeches.

Between February and August, the state issued around 2,000 hunting shirts, and the same number of coats, waistcoats and jackets to its infantry and artillery regiments. For the purpose of accountability, on 31 July 1777, the Massachusetts Board of War defined a suit of clothes as a hat, coat, jacket, breeches, shirt, a pair of stockings and a pair of shoes.

The Massachusetts Line was not arranged until 1779, therefore no regimental breakdown by number is practical for 1777–78. Known uniform details are as follows: Bailey's – at Dorchester on 28 September 1778, an officer requested a blue coat lined white, white or buff facings, plain white buttons and white waistcoat and breeches. On 10 November 1778, 358 suits of imported brown faced red coats and white waistcoats and breeches were received; Greaton's – uniforms were brown faced white in 1777; Rufus Putnam's – from November 1778 uniforms of blue turned-up white, with white lining were to be worn; Thomas Nixon's – on 21 February 1778, the Public Store, Albany, received 340 coats, 18 drummers' and fifers' coats, 340 pairs of breeches, 309 waistcoats, ten green and blue jackets, 50 shirts, and 100 pairs of hose; Ichabod Alden's – received at Albany on 31 January 1778 were 200 coats, 20 waistcoats, 200 pairs of breeches, 199 shirts, 203 pairs of shoes, 99 pairs of hose, on 15 February, 35 caps, on 2 October 1777, 186 milled caps, and on 4 November 1778 300 imported brown faced red uniforms and white waistcoats and breeches; Michael Jackson's – on 2

Deputy Quartermaster General Morgan Lewis, Northern Department, unattributed. Appointed 12 September 1776, Lewis served throughout the war. He is shown here in a blue coat without collar, scarlet lapels, white waistcoat and shirt ruffles. (The Society of the Cincinnati Museum, Anderson House, Washington DC)

November 1777, James Keith received 18 pairs of blue breeches. The following year he received 277 imported brown faced red uniforms, white waistcoats and breeches; James Wesson's – Captain Nahoum Ward died on 6 March 1778 owing for a red coat faced white, on 10 November 1778, 332 suits of imported brown faced red uniforms and white waistcoats and breeches were received; Thomas Marshall's – on 9 November 1778, they received 255 imported blue faced red uniforms and white waistcoats and breeches; Ebenezer Francis's, later Benjamin Tupper's – on 9 November 1778, the unit received 334 imported blue faced red uniforms and white waistcoats and breeches; Gamaliel Bradford's – deserter reports of 1777 indicate a scarlet coat faced black, leather breeches and a beaver hat; on November 1778, the unit received 278 imported suits of blue faced red, and white waistcoats and breeches; Massachusetts State Train of Artillery – blue faced red, blue waistcoats and breeches. Officers' coats were trimmed with gold lace edged lapels and button holes; white watch coats.

New Hampshire

On 21 January 1778, a New Hampshire Board of War was established to supply the Continental regiments with clothing and other necessities. During March 1778, the Board of War sent to Exeter green serge to be made into coats, waistcoats and breeches. On 30 May, 25 June and 29 July, 805 hats, 501 pairs of leather breeches, 229 blankets, 925 shirts, 56 pairs of hose, 493 pairs of overalls, 148 waistcoats, 105 rifle frocks, 885 pairs of shoes, and various amounts of cloth were despatched. The results of the Board of War effort are illustrated in Figure 2, Plate G. In addition to clothing, the state made a green and a blue silk colour for the 1st and 2nd regiments during 1778. The 1st regiment lost its white suit of colours in 1777.

On 16 November 1778, the New Hampshire Regiments received their most complete supply of uniforms consisting of 1,105 imported coats of brown faced red, 1,105 imported waistcoats, pairs of breeches, shirts and pairs of lead coloured hose.

Pennsylvania

Having successfully uniformed its battalions for 1776, Pennsylvania turned to the Continental Clothier General for uniforms. As of 23 September 1777, James Mease reported to General Washington that the 12 Pennsylvania Line regiments plus Colonel Walter Stewart's State regiment had received: 3,915 coats, 4,927 vests, 3,552 pairs of breeches, 9,153 pairs of shoes, 7,600 pairs of hose, 5,588 shirts, 2,328 hats or caps, 674 hunting shirts and 7,045 pairs of overalls. Yet shortages persisted. When, on 6 November, Mease was visited at Lancaster by the

Colonel John Cox, Assistant Quartermaster General, after a miniature by Charles Willson Peale, taken at Valley Forge on 2 March 1778. He wears a blue coat, off-white facings, gilt epaulettes and buttons. (Peter F. Copeland)

commanders of the 5th, 8th, and 10th regiments, he was unable to comply with their requisitions. As a result, the officers bought enough cloth to make 550 coats: 100 brown faced white, 100 blue faced white, 300 blue faced red, and 50 brown faced green.

A 3rd Pennsylvania Regiment receipt book credits the regiment with 254 coats – 200 blue and red, 27 blue and white, 23 red, two white and blue and two sergeants' red regimental. It also lists quantities of blue cloth breeches and waistcoats. By 21 November 1778, Brigadier-general Anthony Wayne's division received new clothing, bound its hats with white and used buckstail for cockades.

The officers of the Pennsylvania Line were among the first to be taken care of by their home state. After December 1777, officers who could claim arrears in clothing could draw, at state expense, superfine broad cloth of brown, blue, claret or other colours, a pair of cotton stockings, a pair of worsted stockings, one pair of fine shoes, a shirt, a stock, two dozen small gilt buttons, shalloon, mohair and linen.

Blue silk standard with the gold embroidered unit designation of the 2nd South Carolina Regiment of the Continental Line. It was presented to the regiment on 1 July 1776 at Charleston, SC. Captured on 9 October 1779 during the Siege of Savannah, it is now in the United States. (Smithsonian Institution)

In May 1777, the State Clothier provided Thomas Proctor's Artillery Regiment with 200 drilling jackets, 200 pairs of shoes, 200 shirts, 200 pairs of hose, 100 pairs of shoes and 100 pairs of buckskin breeches. On 14 July, the State Treasurer paid a bill from Philip Heyd, a Philadelphia tailor, for 13 red regimental coats for the band at 25 shillings per coat. Proctor also contracted with the Pennsylvania Commissary, James Mease, for 100 regimental coats.

New Jersey

Like Pennsylvania, New Jersey turned to the Continental Clothier General for uniforms. On 9 May 1777, James Mease informed Colonel Dayton, on the road from Boston, that he had addressed to the 3rd Regiment 325 blue coats faced red and 12 red coats faced blue for the drums and fifes. Mease had already sent 104 blue coats which were different from the old regimental uniform illustrated in Figure 1 Plate C. These coats were found by George Measam in the Fishkill, New York, clothing store in June 1778.

On 22 May 1778, the New Jersey Council of Safety appointed Major Enos Kelsey commissioner for purchasing clothing for the state's Continental troops. His main responsibility was to buy flax to make into linen. Lieutenant Colonel Israel Shreve of the 2nd New Jersey bought cloth for all New Jersey Continental Line officers and blue breeches for his own regiment. The Israel Shreve Papers at Rutgers University Library contain a receipt dated March 1778 signed by Lt. Derick Lane, for broad cloth in blue, claret and black, red shalloon, brown durant and scarlet. The quantities translate into a blue coat faced in scarlet and lined with red shalloon. The claret coloured cloth might have been used for the waistcoat and breeches, and the rest to make an overcoat. Getting the New Jersey Line into a single uniform took until 1779. The New Jersey State troops – two regional artillery companies – only received hats from the commissioners. The militia light horse officers may have had blue regimental coats turned-up with red and blue saddle clothes edged with white, like the suit advertised by John I. Schenk in the *Pennsylvania Gazette* of 17 March 1778.

New York

With the help of the Continental Clothier at Albany and the efforts of Peter Courtenius, New York clothed its five regiments during 1777. According to a return dated 15 November 1777, John Henry, Commissary of Clothing, accounted to the New York Line for the following: white or check linen and flannel shirts, 4,017 shoes, 4,662 stockings, 3,466 overalls and trousers, 2,425 hats and bonnets, 1,692 upper and under vests, 1,109 pairs of leather and cloth breeches, and 2,675 frocks. George Measam's provision of regimental coats to the New York regiments proved ample until 21 August 1778, when New York's Governor, George Clinton, ordered Henry to issue substantial quantities of every article of clothing for the five regiments.

1st Regiment

In 1777 at Albany the regiment was supplied: 131 drab coats, 30 short blue coats, four brown coats, six grey ratteen short coats, 160 short ratteen coats, 77 swanskin jackets, two crimson and 97 pairs of everlasting breeches and 18 hats; in August 1778, Governor Clinton ordered a suit of clothes for each officer and enlisted man, the officers' regimentals being blue turned-up with red.

2nd Regiment

In 1777 at Albany the regiment was supplied: five hats, 242 coats, 158 waistcoats, six pairs of breeches, 95 shirts, 270 pairs of hose, 46 pairs of shoes, 242 caps, 248 mittens and 105 blankets; on 10 March 1777, Colonel Philip Van Cortlandt wrote that he hoped the New York Convention would provide his regiment with colours corresponding to his uniform of scarlet with white lappets; in 1778 regimental deserters wore brown-sleeved jackets, black breeches, white woollen stockings and round hats.

rd Regiment

n 1777 at Albany the regiment was supplied: 467 coats, 34 pairs of breeches, 256 shirts, 420 stocks, 436 pairs of hose, 82 shoes, 400 caps, 400 mittens, 133 blankets, and $568\frac{1}{2}$ yards of cloth, including 60 blue coats with red facings and white lining, and hats; on 16 March 1778, at Albany a further 225 pairs of shoes, 36 pairs of hose, 297 rifle shirts, 7 dozen buttons and 40 pairs of breeches were supplied. Colonel Gansevoort's regimental coat is illustrated in the pictures on pages 17 and 39.

th Regiment

Between 19 June 1777 and 30 May 1778, Captain Nathan Strong's company received 24 coats, 28 hats, 26 pairs of breeches, 30 stockings, 48 frocks, 48 overalls, and 51 pairs of shoes; in August 1778, a deserter wore a brown homespun coat and jacket with linen overalls. For further detail see Figure 1, Plate G.

Front and rear views of the regimental coat of Colonel Peter Gansevoort, 3rd New York Regiment of the Continental Line, 1777–79. Blue wool with red cape, lapels, cuffs, and front edge of skirts and pockets, white lining and turnbacks. Non-military silver buttons, with raised milled oval on ivory or bone back and quatrefoil button shank indicator. (Gansevoort-Lansing Collection, Smithsonian Institution)

Delaware

With only one Continental battalion, Delaware relied upon the uniforms left over from 1776, to which yellow hat lace was added as a regimental distinction. At the end of 1777, Lieutenant Colonel Charles Pope was sent to Delaware by General Washington to re-clothe the regiment for the coming year. A clothing factory at Newark, established by State Clothier Thomas Rodney, made shirts from linen and 250 pairs of breeches from brown drilling. In June 1778, 19 seamstresses made 427 shirts for the regiment, and on 17 December 1778, the Delaware Assembly voted to instruct the State Clothier General to provide each officer with a coat, a waistcoat and a pair of breeches, or, in lieu, the sum of £80 for past services.

Virginia

In 1777 Virginia's Continental regiments converted from hunting shirts to regimental coats. To induce the Virginia Line to reinforce Washington, the Continental Congress promised to supply sufficient scarlet cloth to face their clothes. Detachments of Virginia troops joined the Army partially uniformed by their home state and hoping to have their uniform completed on arrival in camp, with round hats with two inch brims, prescribed the previous winter in Williamsburg.

In January 1778, Virginia's 15 regiments, consisting of 4,465 rank and file present or fit for duty, were credited with 6,211 coats issued by the Clothier General. State cloth imported from France on the Virginia state sloop *Congress* was deposited at Lancaster on 2 December 1777 and handed to Virginia agents to be made into clothing. With the cloth in hand, Brigadier General George Weedon excused from duty the tailors in his 2nd Virginia Brigade to make up the clothing. On 29 December 1777, Weedon recommended to Washington that the uniform should be a short coat, cuffed and caped in different colours, a short waistcoat without shirts, a small round hat, black leather or hair stocks, and overalls in both summer and winter. Mease had such a uniform – drab coloured country-made cloth with scarlet cuffs and collar – made at Lancaster in March for the 9th Virginia.

Other uniforms of the Virginia Continental regiments were: 1st, blue faced scarlet; 2nd, blue faced blue and white button holes; 3rd, pale blue coats faced blue, and green waistcoats; 4th, blue coats, white breeches and waistcoats; 5th, purple linen coats; 6th, blue coats and brown small clothes; 7th, brown faced scarlet; 8th, blue coats and buff small clothes; 12th blue turned-up white; 13th, blue cuffed yellow and blue breeches; 14th, white hunting shirts; 15th, brown faced buff.

Device of the regimental standard of the 2nd South Carolina Regiment of the Continental Line. A tree trunk is topped by a red liberty cap, one blue and one faded red standard, a buff coloured drum, the motto in gold 'Vita potior libertas' and the year '1775'. The wreath on one side has acorns and on the other small white flowers. (Smithsonian Institution)

At the end of 1778, the Virginia Public Store in Philadelphia sold the officers cloth for a blue or brown faced scarlet uniform. Virginia's state regulars were uniformed as follows: 1st State Regiment – blue coats, striped jackets, drilling breeches, caps with bands and buckles, and white shalloon camp colours; 2nd State Regiment – blue or brown coats turned-up and lined red, caps as 1st Regiment; State Artillery Regiment – blue coats, red lapels and cuffs, red lining and small clothes, cocked hats and yellow buttons; State Garrison Regiment as State Artillery Regiment but white buttons; French Company – blue coats, scarlet lapels, buff breeches and waistcoats; State Laboratory – blue suits and check shirts; Volunteer Cavalry – blue coats edged white, white waistcoats, leather breeches, and hats with black feathers.

Maryland

Due to the lack of clothing for the seven regiments of Maryland troops, Washington despatched Lieutenant Colonel Adams to buy clothing in Maryland with $2,000 to be drawn from the Continental Paymaster. Acting on this request, Governor Johnson appointed clothing agents across the state to buy up cloth, clothing and blankets. By the end of 1777, Maryland's Continental troops were issued with 137 regimental suits, 692 coats, 723 vests, 279 pairs of breeches, 539 hats, 79 hunting shirts, 696 overalls and 1,974 shirts.

The capture in Wilmington, Delaware, of a brig laden with the baggage of three British regiments, and the later despatch of James Calhoun, of Baltimore, as state clothier at camp, covered the Maryland Line for 1778. By this time, the uniform had been established as blue coats faced red with white waistcoats and breeches. The troops at Wilmington also converted captured British goods into scarlet waistcoats and breeches. The 4th Regiment wore brown coats procured in Baltimore by Colonel Samuel Smith, and reserved the blue faced red coats for drums and fifes.

North Carolina

In August 1777, a 10th Regiment and an artillery company were added to the state's Continental quota. For the original nine regiments, the only additions in 1777 to the uniforms that were received at the end of 1776 were 679 coats and a proportion of other articles, delivered by the Clothier General.

Governor Richard Caswell, following the rules laid out by the Continental Clothier General, sent to James Mease over 4,000 yards of blue, brown, green and white woollen cloth, 300 blankets, 1,500 yards of osnaburg and shoes and stockings that had been destined for the North Carolina regiments during 1778. At Kingston in February, officers received blue cloth, red facings and gilt buttons. The rank

Colonel George Baylor, 3rd Regiment of Continental Light Dragoons, miniature taken by Charles Willson Peale at Valley Forge in the Spring of 1778. White uniform, stock and ruffles, dark blue lapels and cape edged in silver, silver buttons, epaulettes, and belt buckle; black sword belt. (The Society of the Cincinnati Museum, Anderson House, Washington DC)

and file received brown cloth, red facings and white buttons. The 10th North Carolina (see Figure 3, Plate G) was clothed from the Virginia Public Store. Recruits enlisted in April 1778 for nine months to fill the state's Continental regiments were to have a bounty suit provided by their home militia, this consisted of a hunting shirt, a sleeved waistcoat, one pair of breeches, shoes, stockings, two shirts, and a hat.

South Carolina

During 1777–78, South Carolina continued to clothe its regiments without Continental supplies. It even sent its own representative, Commodore Alexander Gillon, to France to negotiate imports of fabrics. On 30 January 1778, the firm of Lozy and D'Lombard received at

Colonel Thomas Crafts, Massachusetts State Train of Artillery, after an unattributed miniature. Blue faced scarlet uniform worn by the regiment until 1779. Lace, epaulettes and buttons are gold; white waistcoat and stock. (Peter F. Copeland)

CONCLUSION

From April 1775 to the end of 1778, the uniforms of General Washington's armies changed considerably. At the beginning of the rebellion, only the independent companies and some minute militia companies reported in uniform. However most rebelling provinces quickly initiated efforts to clothe their troops. While many uniforms were made available, little standardisation could be achieved due to the lack of a general clothing warrant, and conflicts between Congress and the states over local purchases and the importation of materials.

Although hunting shirts were initially ordered as uniform by New Jersey, Maryland, Virginia and North Carolina, and favoured by Washington and the Continental Congress, by the end of 1777, the preferred uniform was the regimental coat. However, no standardisation of colour was achieved. Among the 22,586 coats known to have been issued during 1777, blue, black, grey, drab, green, red, brown and white are all recorded, and even with the arrival from France in late 1778 of over 20,000 brown and blue coats, complete uniformity was still elusive.

Charleston and sold to South Carolina: 4,217 yards of blue and 643 yards of buff wool, and 10,339 yards of white cadix and tricot cloth.

Changes in uniform principally affected the 3rd Regiment. This began life as a mounted riflemen unit and was transformed into an infantry unit with Charleville muskets, blue coats faced scarlet, white buttons, black cocked hats laced black, white small clothes and French full-length white leggings. See Figure 3, Plate E, for the uniform of the 4th Regiment.

Georgia

Georgia's four Continental regiments had locally made uniforms that consisted of short waistcoats over jackets, kilts worn over overalls and Kilmarnock caps. General orders of 21 May 1778 prescribe the camp colours each battalion was allowed: 1st, blue field with yellow insertions; 2nd, white and blue; 3rd, green and white; and 4th, red and blue. Portraits of Joseph Habersham of the 1st Georgia Battalion and Major Joseph Woodruff of the Georgia Artillery show officers in proper regimental coats. Habersham is in a blue coat faced, cuffed and caped in yellow, a yellow waistcoat, a white egret plume in his hat, and a gilt gorget with a coiled rattlesnake engraved on it. See Figure 2, Plate E, for the artillery uniform.

Select Bibliography

Published Works

Walter Clark (edit), *The State Records of North Carolina* (Raleigh 1886–), vols. 11–13.

Donald H. Cresswell (comp.), *The American Revolution in Drawings and Prints, a checklist of 1765–1790 graphics in the Library of Congress* (Washington DC, 1975)

Georgia Historical Society, *Collections* (Savannah 1902), vol. 5.

Philip M. Hamer (edit), *The Papers of Henry Laurens* (Columbia, SC 1968–), vols. 12, 13.

Hugh Hastings (edit), *Public Papers of George Clinton, First Governor of New York 1777–1795* (Albany 1900), vols. II and III.

Charles H. Lesser (edit), *The Sinews of Independence Monthly Strength Reports of the Continental Army* (Chicago 1976).

Captain Fitzhugh McMaster, *Soldiers and Uniforms: South Carolina Military Affairs 1670–1775* (Columbia, SC 1971).

William James Morgan (edit), *Naval Documents of the American Revolution* (Washington DC), 9 vols.

E. B. O'Callaghan (edit), *Documents Relative to the Colonial History of the State of New York* (Albany 1857) vol. 8.

Edward W. Richardson, *Standards and Colours of the American Revolution* (1982).

Erna Risch, *Supplying Washington's Army* (Washington DC 1981).

William L. Saunders (edit), *Colonial Records of North Carolina* (Raleigh, NC 1890), vol. 10.

Charles Coleman Sellers, *Portraits and Miniatures by Charles Willson Peale* (Philadelphia 1952) and *Charles Willson Peale With Patron and Populace* (Philadelphia 1969).

Richard K. Showman (edit), *The Papers of General Nathanael Greene* (Chapel Hill, NC 1976), vols. 1, 2.

Robert G. Stewart, *Henry Benbridge (1743–1812) American Portrait Painter* (Washington 1971).

John B. B. Trussell Jr., *The Pennsylvania Line Regimental Organization and Operations, 1776–1783* (Harrisburg 1977).

William B. Wilcox (edit), *The Papers of Benjamin Franklin* (New Haven 1983), vols. 23 and 24.

Robert K. Wright Jr., *The Continental Army* (Washington, DC 1983).

The Company of Military Collectors and Historians series: *Military Uniforms in America* (cited as MUIA) and *Military Collector and Historian, passim.*

Manuscripts

US National Archives: Record Group 360, M247, *Papers of the Continental Congress,*(1774–1789) *passim.*; Record Group 93, M859, *Miscellaneous numbered records (The Manuscript File) in the War Department collection of Revolutionary War Records passim.*; M853, *Numbered record books concerning military operations and service, pay and settlement of accounts and supplies in the War Department collection of Revolutionary War Records passim.*; Virginia State Library, Archives Division, Williamsburg Public Store, *Daybooks* and *Journals* (1776–1778); US Library of Congress, *George Washington Papers*, series 4, rolls 33–55, series 5, rolls 115–117; *Peter Force Historical Manuscripts*, series 9, boxes 9–34; New York Historical Society, *The Horatio Gates Papers* (1726–1828), rolls 3–8, 20; *Day Book of John Tayler, Storekeeper, Albany* (January 1776–April 1777); *Duer papers, vol. 1*; *New York Public Library, Gansevoort-Lansing Papers*, box 21; New York State Archives, *New York State Accounts Audited*, vol. A; *Philip Van Rensselaer Papers of the Historic Cherry Hill Papers*, Acct. No. SC14764; New Jersey State Archives, Department of Defence Records and numbered records 9930–10699; Rutgers University Libraries, *Papers of Israel Shreve, Papers of Gershom Mott*; Connecticut State Library and Archives, series 1–3, military records 1775–1778, *Jonathan Trumbull Collection*; Yale University Library, *Deacon Nathan Beers Collection*; Maryland Hall of Records, *Maryland State Papers (Series D, Revolutionary War Papers)*; Massachusetts Archives, *Board of War*

Major Nicholas Rogers, aide-de-camp, after a portrait by Charles Willison Peale, taken in October 1778. Rogers wears a blue coat with buff lapels and pointed cuffs, gold buttons and epaulettes, and green silk ribbon. Note the unusual lapels, these should be compared to the portrait of Colonel George Baylor which appears on page 41 and the lapelettes mentioned in the order for the uniforms of the 1st Continental Light Dragoons, see page 20. Note also the double-breasted waistcoat. (Peter F. Copeland)

Papers, Revolution Council Papers, Revolutionary War Rolls (all *passim.*); Massachusetts Historical Society, *Papers of William Heath*, rolls 6–11, *Miscellaneous Bound Volume 15, 1776–1778*; New Hampshire Archives, Record Group 7, *Military Records – Colonial Period*, boxes 2–11; American Philosophical Society Library, *Papers of Benjamin Franklin*, vols. 42, 61; Historical Society of Pennsylvania, *Papers of Anthony Wayne*, vols. 1, 2; *William Irvine Papers*, vol. 1; *Cadwalader Collection, General John Cadwalader Section*; Pennsylvania Historic and Museum Commission, RG 27 records of Pennsylvania's Revolutionary governments 1775–1790, *Board of War Minutes 1777*, RG 28 records of the Treasury Department, *State Store Journal 1776–1777*; Brown University, Anne S. K. Brown Military Collection, *Miscellaneous Papers of Henry*

Jackson; Rhode Island State Archives, vols. 7–16, 18, *Letters to the Governor*, vols 3, 8, 10–12; University of Virginia Microfilm, *Lee Family Papers 1742–1785*, rolls 3–5.

THE PLATES

A1: Private, Lower Regiment of New Castle, Delaware Militia, 1775–1776

The field officers of the militia agreed that the upper, middle and lower regiments should be uniformed in short light blue coats, lined white, with slash pockets and false slash sleeves, plain small white buttons and button holes on each side of the breast, short white belted waistcoats, white breeches, black garters, white stockings and half spatter-dashes; small round hats, without button or loop, bound black with a ribbon around the crown the colour of the facings. The upper regiment wore cuffs and capes of white, the middle wore buff, and the lower wore green. (*Delaware Archives.*)

A2: Grenadier, Captain John Lasher's New York City Grenadier Company, 1775–76

See the portrait on page 4 for further detail. The motto on the cap is adapted from the text found on the German Fusiliers' pouches. (*MUIA Plate No. 562.*)

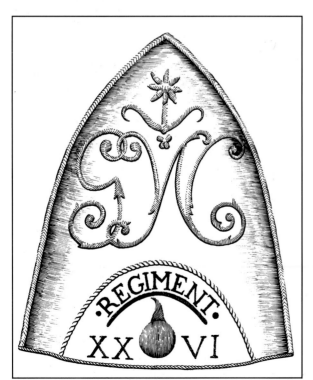

A3: Captain Benedict Arnold, Governor's Second Company of Guards, Connecticut, 1775

On 28 December 1774, 65 New Haven gentlemen agreed to form themselves into a volunteer company. On 2 February 1775 they voted that the dress of the company be 'a scarlet coat of common length, the lapels, cuffs and collar of buff, and trimmed with plain silver wash buttons, white linen vest, breeches and stockings, black half-leggings, a small fashionable and narrow [hat]'. After petitioning the General Assembly to be named 'Governor's Second Company of Guards', they were mustered into the 2nd Regiment of Militia of the Colony, and Benedict Arnold was named Captain. (*History of the City of New Haven*, New York 1885, pp. 649–650.)

A4: Colonel John Cadwalader, 3rd Battalion Philadelphia Associators, 1775–76

Colonel Cadwalader's uniforms were made on 20 May and 7 September 1775 and included a $\frac{1}{4}$ of a yard of white cloth for cuffs and lapels, 38 coat and 36 vest buttons, white dimity for vest and breeches, black silk garters, white taffeta facings, a blue striped saddle cloth, black bearskin holsters, a round hat, rose and band, two silver epaulettes with bullion fringe, and an eagle head silver mounted hanger with black ebony handle and chains. (General John Cadwalader Section, Cadwalader Collection, Historical Society of Pennsylvania.)

B1: Grenadier, 26th Continental Regiment of Foot, 1776

Regimental commander Colonel Loami Baldwin listed a London brown coat of uniform with epaulettes, light blue jacket and white breeches in his invoice of clothing dated 10 June 1776. Members of the regiment claimed for losses of grenadier caps and coats. (Revolutionary War Rolls, Vol. 58, Massachusetts Archives; David Library of the American Revolution.)

B2: Rifleman, 1st Continental Regiment of Foot, 1776

Colonel Edward Hand ordered 2,000 yards of linen for frocks and trousers for 624 men. This was to be dyed green and trimmed in red. (*Papers of Edward Hand*, Vol. 1, f. and box, Historical Society of Pennsylvania.)

Grenadier mitre cap, 26th Continental Infantry Regiment, 1776. Reconstruction based on D. W. Holst's analysis of thread holes showing the probable arrangement of the damaged portion of the front flap revealing a pattern of Roman numerals 'XXVI'. (Smithsonian photograph)

B3: Chaplain William Emerson, 2nd Continental Regiment of Foot, 1776

On his way to join his regiment as chaplain, the Rev. William Emerson asked his wife to turn and face his blue coat with black. This coat, along with a black cloak, black jacket and breeches, beaver hat, and sword, was included in the inventory of his estate. (*Diaries and Letters of William Emerson 1743–1776* (n.p., 1972), pp. 105, 127.)

C1: Corporal, 3rd New Jersey Battalion, 1776

In April 1776, three deserters from Captain John Moss's Company were advertised in the *Pennsylvania Packet* wearing new hats bound with white, new regimental coats of drab faced with blue, buckskin breeches, new shirts and shoes. A portrait of Major Joseph Bloomfield by Charles Willson Peale shows pointed cuffs, slash sleeves with four small buttons and silver shoulder knots.

C2: Captain, Light Infantry Company, 2nd South Carolina Regiment, 1776–78

According to regimental orders of 20 June 1775, every officer was to provide himself with a blue coatee, faced, cuffed and lined scarlet, white buttons, white waistcoat and breeches, a black cap and black feather. The lapels were narrow and the $\frac{5}{8}$ inch white metal buttons were stamped with a '2'. This figure is based on Henry Benbridge's posthumous portrait of Captain Charles Motte, who fell in the Siege of Savannah in 1779. (*MUIA Plate No. 450.*)

C3: Corporal, 6th Virginia Regiment, 1776–77

On 2 August 1776, Colonel Mordecai Buckner ordered the regiment to adopt the following uniform: short, hanging just below the waistband of the breeches, brown oznabrig hunting shirts faced on collar and cuffs with red, drummers' and fifers' shirts were white with brown cuffs; corporals to have red twist shoulder knots. From the Virginia Public Store, the regiment received blue duffel cloth for leggings and striped cloth for breeches and waistcoats. Hats had a two inch wide brim with black ribbon binding and were cocked up on the left side. *Orderly Book, 6th Virginia Regiment, 1776–1778*, Americana Collection, National Society Daughters of the American Revolution.)

D1: Trooper, 4th Continental Light Dragoons, 1777–78

General Washington allowed the Clothier General to issue 40 red faced blue coats of the 8th and 21st Foot to the 4th Light Dragoons. Orange coloured hunting shirts concealed the red coats; black leather breeches and British-style leather helmets. (*George Washington Papers*, Series 4; *Revolutionary War Rolls*, jacket 14, roll 115.)

Captain Daniel Parker, 3rd Continental Artillery Regiment, unattributed. Parker resigned his commission on 3 October 1778, but his coat appears to be blue rather than black. Lapels and cape are red, as is the backing to the epaulette which is of gold lace to match the buttons. A gold welt edges the white waistcoat; white cravat and ruffles. (Photo by James Kochan, Morristown National Historical Park)

D2: Captain Samuel Chandler, 11th Connecticut Militia Regiment, Light Horse Company, 1776/7

He wears a blue frock coat with gold epaulettes, a white waistcoat trimmed with gold lace, white breeches and a gold laced hat. Based on Captain Chandler's portrait by Joseph Chandler, National Gallery, Washington DC.

D3: Trumpeter, 1st Continental Light Dragoons

This figure wears a green faced brown tunic with a brown fringe hanging from the shoulders, white belts, brown trumpet banners, black caps with green turbans and yellow tassels.

E1: Matross, 1st Company of Maryland Artillery, 1776

Deserters from Captain Nathaniel Smith's Company of Artillery wore new felt hats with white loops, white pewter buttons marked 'MM1' vertically, blue regimental coats turned-up with light grey, grey waistcoats, leather breeches and blue yarn stockings. (*Maryland Journal and Baltimore Advertiser*, 1 May and 14 August 1776; *Maryland State Papers*.)

E2: Captain, Georgia Artillery, 1778
The uniform of black coat, scarlet lapels and cape, gilt buttons and epaulette conforms to that of the Continental Artillery. The white waistcoat with heavy gold lace and buttons and the red egret feather are shown in a portrait of Major Joseph Woodruff of the Georgia Artillery.

E3: Gunner, 4th South Carolina Regiment, Artillery, 1775–78
Men of this regiment wore blue coats with small standing collars and red tabs and lapels, dragoon sleeves and angular cuffs; blue breeches and waistcoats were worn in winter, white in summer. Hair was cut for wearing with caps. (*MUIA Plate No. 485*, and Henry Benbridge's painting, *Death of Colonel Owen Roberts*.)

F1: Private, Thomas Hartley's Additional Continental Regiment of Foot, 1778
Hartley informed General Washington he had ordered uniforms of blue faced white cut in the style of 'His Excellency's' uniform; caps were also ordered. (George Washington Papers, roll 40.)

F2: Private, Henry Jackson's Additional Continental Regiment of Foot, 1777
Colonel Jackson obtained in Boston British accoutrements and arms and a uniform of blue and buff, lined white, white waistcoat and breeches and large hats with white binding. (Colonel Henry Jackson to Messrs Otis and Andrews, Camp Pautuxet, 14 October, 1778, Anne S. K. Brown Military Collection, Providence, Rhode Island.)

F3: Ensign, Samuel Blatchley Webb's Additional Continental Regiment of Foot, 1777
In 1777 the regiment obtained captured British uniforms which were faced with white then changed to yellow in 1778, with white waistcoats and breeches. (Samuel Blatchley Webb Papers, series 2, box 12, folder 8, Yale University.)

G1: Private, 4th New York Regiment of the Continental Line, 1778
As his officers had already obtained this uniform, in September 1778 Colonel Henry B. Livingston requested suits of white regimentals turned-up and lined with scarlet caps with black hair, black knee garters, black or scarlet stocks, and brass knee and shoe buckles. (Dreer Collection series 51:1, p.72, Historical Society of Pennsylvania.)

G2: Fifer, 1st New Hampshire Regiment of the Continental Line, 1778
On 30 May 1778, New Hampshire's Commissary of Military Stores shipped to Valley Forge: 12 yellow regimental coats, 12 pairs of green breeches and 12 jacket for the drummers and fifers of the 1st and 3rd regiments (Commissary Papers, box 3, RG 12, New Hampshire Records and Archives.)

G3: Private, 10th North Carolina Regiment of the Continental Line, 1778
This soldier, like many of his comrades, has no footwear and his feet have become covered with mud. His uniform has also seen better days, the blue faced green coat ha

Reconstruction of the imported coat of 1778. Over 20,000 coats made in France were received by the Continental Army during 1778. (Peter F. Copeland)

Fragment of New Standard Number 1 for the Army of the United States. This standard corresponds to the first of 13 'New' standards with division colours recorded as being held in the Continental Store in mid-1778. The full return is in the US National Archives. It has a green ground, mixed from a pale blue warp and a pale yellow weft. It is 70 inches on the hoist, and around 78 inches on the fly. There are 13 stars in the circular form of the Union. (Collections of the Division of Armed Forces History, National Museum of American History, Smithsonian Institution.)

become faded and worn, as has his hat. His ragged appearance is typical of many Continental units during the harsh winter at Valley Forge.

H1: Private, Light Infantry Company, 2nd Canadian Regiment, 1777–78
This private wears a brown coat with white cuffs and

buttons, and a white waistcoat. Hanging from the crossbelt of his cartridge pouch is a picker and brush for cleaning the flintlock he carries over his shoulder.

H2: Private, 2nd Rhode Island State Regiment, 1777–78
Deserters from the regiment wore blue sailors' jackets,

small round hats and striped flannel overalls. (*Providence Gazette*, 3 January, 1778.)

H3: Dragoon, Pulaski's Legion, 1778

The appearance of Pulaski's legion owed much to the unit's Polish origins and the efforts of General Count Pulaski. The dragoon illustrated here wears a short blue coat with bound frogged button holes in the Polish manner. His cap is decorated with grey fur. He leans on his lance and carries his musket slung over his shoulder.

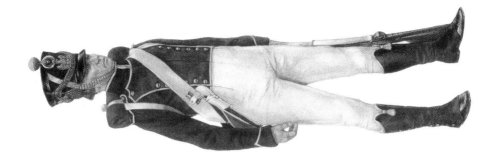

OSPREY PUBLISHING

FIND OUT MORE ABOUT OSPREY

❏ Please send me a FREE trial issue
of Osprey Military Journal

❏ Please send me the latest listing of Osprey's publications

❏ I would like to subscribe to Osprey's e-mail newsletter

Title/rank _____

Name _____

Address _____

_____

_____

Postcode/zip _____ state/country _____

e-mail _____

Which book did this card come from?

_____

❏ I am interested in military history

My preferred period of military history is _____

❏ I am interested in military aviation

My preferred period of military aviation is _____

I am interested in (please tick all that apply)

❏ general history   ❏ militaria   ❏ model making
❏ wargaming   ❏ re-enactment

Please send to:

USA & Canada: Osprey Direct USA, c/o Motorbooks
International, P.O. Box 1, 729 Prospect Avenue, Osceola,
WI 54020

UK, Europe and rest of world:
Osprey Direct UK, P.O. Box 140, Wellingborough, Northants,
NN8 2FA, United Kingdom

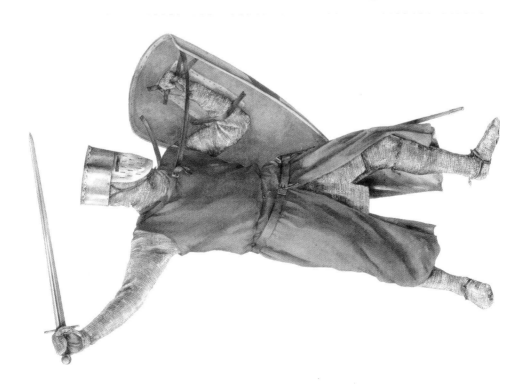

OSPREY
PUBLISHING

www.ospreypublishing.com

call our telephone hotline
for a free information pack

USA & Canada: 1-800-458-0454
UK, Europe and rest of world call:
+44 (0) 1933 443 863

Young Guardsman
Figure taken from *Warrior 22:
Imperial Guardsman 1799–1815*
Published by Osprey
Illustrated by Christa Hook

Knight, c.1190
Figure taken from *Warrior 1: Norman Knight 950 – 1204AD*
Published by Osprey
Illustrated by Christa Hook

POSTCARD